Swan Song

A Thriller

Norman Robbins

A SAMUEL FRENCH ACTING EDITION

SAMUEL FRENCH

FOUNDED 1830

SAMUELFRENCH.COM
SAMUELFRENCH-LONDON.CO.UK

FOR PRODUCTION ENQUIRIES

UNITED STATES AND CANADA

Info@SamuelFrench.com

1-866-598-8449

UNITED KINGDOM AND EUROPE

Plays@SamuelFrench-London.co.uk

020-7255-4302

Each title is subject to availability from Samuel French, depending upon country of performance. Please be aware that *SWAN SONG* may not be licensed by Samuel French in your territory. Professional and amateur producers should contact the nearest Samuel French office or licensing partner to verify availability.

MUSIC USE NOTE

Licensees are solely responsible for obtaining formal written permission from copyright owners to use copyrighted music in the performance of this play and are strongly cautioned to do so. If no such permission is obtained by the licensee, then the licensee must use only original music that the licensee owns and controls. Licensees are solely responsible and liable for all music clearances and shall indemnify the copyright owners of the play(s) and their licensing agent, Samuel French, against any costs, expenses, losses and liabilities arising from the use of music by licensees. Please contact the appropriate music licensing authority in your territory for the rights to any incidental music.

IMPORTANT BILLING AND CREDIT REQUIREMENTS

If you have obtained performance rights to this title, please refer to your licensing agreement for important billing and credit requirements.

CHARACTERS

MARIANNE GRAYSON

TRYPHOSA SWAN

AMY BEVERAGE

FRANK BEVERAGE

CARLA GUNTER-MASON

ANDREW PERRYMAN

SCENE

The action of the play takes place in the living room of "Cooper's View", home of Marianne Grayson, on the outskirts of Durning-on-Tace. near London. Time: 2005

ACT ONE

Scene One : An afternoon in July.
Scene Two : Later that Evening.
Scene Three : Mid morning. Two days later.

ACT TWO

Scene One : Afternoon. Eight days later.
Scene Two : Late the following morning.
Scene Three : A week later. Early afternoon.

AUTHOR'S NOTE

This play was written in response to several requests for a small cast mystery play with good roles for senior actresses. I wasn't entirely sure what a senior actress was, (It all depends on the actress and her learning capabilities in my experience) but decided that 70-80 was a fairly wide range and a 60-70 year old could easily play up, so I drafted out a plot and got to work.

I've been a constant opera-goer since the 1940's, so the idea of a retired Opera singer being involved in a murder mystery is not unusual. *Tosca, Carmen, Rigoletto,* and dozens of other operas feature stabbings, strangulations, drownings, shootings, beheadings, matricides, patricides and suicides, One can count Operatic happy endings almost on one hand. On the downside, however, was the knowledge that not everyone likes (or even understands) opera, so the script had to be very accessible to groups and audiences with absolutely no interest in that form of theatre.

The result is Swan Song. Apart from a few references to real operas and singers, this is simply a murder mystery. The only opera singing comes in the final moment of the play, and there are several commercial recordings of the aria available on CD. It's a beautiful, very melodic soprano showpiece, and only a few bars need to be heard as the final curtain descends. It is, indeed, Tryphosa's swan song.

The title to look for is *Io son l'umile ancella.* (I am a humble servant of the arts) and is from the opera *Adriana Lecouvreur* by Francesco Cilea.

Norman Robbins.

Other plays and pantomimes by Norman Robbins
published by Samuel French

And Evermore Shall Be So
At The Sign of "The Crippled Harlequin"
Aladdin
Ali Baba and the Forty Thieves
Babes in the Wood
The Borzoletti Monstrance
Cinderella
Dick Whittington
The Dragon of Wantley
The Grand Old Duke of York
Hansel and Gretel
Hickory Dickory Dock
Humpty Dumpty
Jack and Jill
Jack and the Beanstalk
The Late Mrs Early
Nightmare
The Old Woman Who Lived in a Shoe
Practice to Deceive
Prepare to Meet Thy Tomb
Prescription for Murder
Pull the Other One
Puss in Boots
Red Riding Hood
Rumpelstiltzkin
Sing a Song of Sixpence
Slaughterhouse
Sleeping Beauty
Snow White
Tiptoe Through the Tombstones
Tom, the Piper's Son
A Tomb with a View
Wedding of the Year
The White Cat
The Wonderful Story of Mother Goose

For Josie Gliddon
who inadvertently inspired the creation of Tryphosa Swan.
"Possente Fhtha."

ACT ONE

Scene One

(An afternoon in July)

(The house was built in the 1830s, and its spacious living room is typical of its kind. The rear wall is dominated by central French windows affording a view of an expansive and well tended garden. Light curtains and a matching pelmet frame the windows. Right of the window is a display cabinet, filled with assorted china, etc., and on top of this, a vase of flowers and assorted framed photographs. Left of the window is an upright piano, obviously dating to the middle of last century, but well polished and cared for. The keyboard cover is down, but an old score of an opera or oratorio is on the music rest. A metronome stands back left, on top of the piano, and an anglepoise lamp, used to illuminate the piano keyboard, is just off centre. A piano bench or stool is tucked beneath the keyboard. An arched opening in the wall left leads to a hall, the front and rear of the house, and the stairs to the upper floor. Below the arch is a long sideboard or table, its surface occupied by matching vases, a ceramic bowl and various knick-knacks. Below this, a stand supporting a leafy plant. Opposite this, on the wall right, an old-fashioned TV set is angled centre stage, and beside this, a magazine rack holding the "TV Times", a recent copy of "Reader's Digest", a "National Geographic" magazine and a newspaper. Upstage of this, a shelved recess supports a music centre, CDs, DVDs, books, ornaments, etc., and towards the back wall, a

small writing desk. On top of this, a table lamp and a few trinkets. A comfortable looking sofa with bright cushions is centre of the room, angled slightly right to give a good view of the television. Matching easy chairs are slightly below this, left and right, angled cf as though facing the room's fireplace. A hearthrug, fire irons, and reversed fender, etc, cf will reinforce the illusion. Behind the sofa is a long, narrow table, and in front of the sofa is a medium sized coffee table. On this a glossy book on gardening. The floor is carpeted, walls warmly decorated with various pictures and portraits as space permits. The light switch is upstage of the arch opening. The whole effect should be comfort, and easy on the eye.)

(When the scene begins, **TRYPHOSA SWAN** *is sitting on the sofa, browsing through a classical music magazine. She is a retired opera singer in her early seventies, and very much a Prima Donna with a sharp tongue, though fortunately this is tempered by a sense of ironic humour. She is elegantly dressed in an exclusive summer trouser suit and blouse and appropriate jewellery. A matching handbag is on the floor, by her feet. After a moment, her face registers amusement as a few words in the magazine catch her attention.)*

TRYPHOSA. *(scornfully)* As *if. (Reads further)* Obviously written by someone who hasn't heard a *real* singer in the last fifty years. *(In disbelief)* Voice of the *Century*? Good God, man. I could have made a better noise with my *bottom.*

*(***MARIANNE GRAYSON*** *enters left, carrying a small tray holding delicate china cups, saucers, milk jug and teapot. She is almost eighty, easygoing by nature, and rather frail. She wears a floral dress and a small pendant necklace.)*

MARIANNE. What was that, dear? I didn't quite catch. *(Depositing the tray on the table behind the sofa.)*

TRYPHOSA. *(airily)* I don't know why you buy this rubbish, Marianne. *You* know more about opera than the moron in this rag. *(Brandishes the magazine)* How he can mention her in the same breath as Tebaldi or Sutherland, I can't imagine. I've a good mind to write to the editor.

MARIANNE. *(preparing the crockery)* Who are we talking about?

TRYPHOSA. *Her,* of course. The one the papers have been oo-ing and ahh-ing about since she won that so-called talent show on television. *(Scornfully)* Vanessa *Rapture.*

MARIANNE. *(non-committally)* Oh.

TRYPHOSA. *Rupture's* more like it. Her upper register's like fingernails on a blackboard. Did you hear her *Casta Diva* in the final? Never mind having my fingers in my ears, I almost buried my arms in them.

MARIANNE. *(mildly)* I can't say I've heard her at all, to be truthful. *(Begins to pour the tea)*

TRYPHOSA. *(dryly)* You haven't missed anything, believe me. Why is it that anyone who sings anything but "pop songs" these days, gets labelled an opera singer? Most of them couldn't do an opera if their life depended on it. *(Regretfully)* When I think of the training *I* had to go through... *(Drops the magazine onto the floor)*

MARIANNE. That was fifty years ago, dear. And the world's a different place, now. *(Adds three lumps of sugar to a cup and passes it to her)*

TRYPHOSA. *(taking it)* All the same...you don't sing *Norma* after a week's coaching with a former chorus member of *Cats.* *(Expanding on the theme)* And that's the trouble, isn't it? There aren't the teachers, any more. People who know voices. Where's today's Borgioli, for instance? Most of the ones *I* come across couldn't tell a Diminuendo from a bout of laryngitis. *(Stirs the tea and sips at it)*

MARIANNE. *(adding one lump of sugar to her own cup and stirring it)* We *do* seem to be having an off-day this morning. Problems at home again? *(Picks up the cup and saucer)*

TRYPHOSA. *(surprised)* No. Why should there be?

MARIANNE. *(moving round to sit beside her)* Well I can't help noticing your vitriolic side emerges every time Carla's in the country. One minute you're Little Mary Sunshine, and the next it's Lucrezia Borgia. Sometimes I have to think twice before wishing you "good morning".

TRYPHOSA. *(indignantly)* Don't be ridiculous. Whenever I'm in this house, I'm as light-hearted as a butterfly. *(Glances around)* I don't know what it *is* about the place, but when you've finally shuffled off the mortal coil, I'm going to sell La Fenice and move in here, lock, stock and barrel. You wouldn't mind that, would you?

MARIANNE. *(mildly)* If I'd already gone, you'd be welcome. I've no family to leave it to. But don't even *think* of doing your Princess de Bouillon act and bumping me off with a bunch of poisoned violets. I know that opera as well as you do. *(Sips at her tea)*

TRYPHOSA. *(remembering)* Ah... *Adrianna Lecouvreur.* *(Brightly)* I sang it in San Francisco, you know. With Carlo Bergonzi. *(Fondly)* Such a *lovely* man.

MARIANNE. *(nodding)* So you told me.

TRYPHOSA. *(remembering)* It was the year I met Lewis. The *first* time, I mean. His company was sponsoring the production, though I'd no idea at the time. It wasn't till the following season...when I returned to do *Boheme*...that the penny dropped. Six months later he proposed *(coyly)* and poor little me became Mrs Lewis Luxmore, fifth richest woman in California.

MARIANNE. And was that when the trouble started? With Carla? *(Sips again)*

TRYPHOSA. *(dismissively)* Oh, no. No. She was a *bitch* from the day she was born. What on earth I'd done to deserve *her*, I can't imagine. Not a bit like her sister. With Carla, it was want, want, want, but with Amy... well...you've already *met* her. Never asked for a thing in her *life*. If it wasn't for that vile husband of hers... *(Breaks off)* Still...we don't want to talk about *them*, do we? I've something *far* more interesting to tell you. *(Sips her tea)* You're going to *love* this. *(Triumphantly)* There's a chance we can trace her.

MARIANNE. *(puzzled)* Who?

TRYPHOSA. My birth mother, of course. A few more days and it shouldn't be a mystery any more. *(Puts the cup and saucer on the coffee table)*

MARIANNE. *(interested)* Really?

TRYPHOSA. Remember when I visited, last time? I told you I'd hired Andrew Perryman from Heritage Research to go into it for me?

MARIANNE. The only thing I remember from last time, was you going on about the call you'd had from Carla and what you were going to *do* about it. You never mentioned an Andrew Perryman. *(Prepares to sip at her tea)*

TRYPHOSA. *(accusingly)* You couldn't have been listening. I've told *everyone* about it. Even that ghastly child from *Celebrity Life* magazine. *(Scornfully)* How she expected to do an in-depth interview with me when she'd never heard me sing, I can't imagine. I'd *retired* before she was born. *(Remembering)* When *Opera* magazine interviewed me in April '86, the reporter knew every...

MARIANNE. *(lowering her cup)* Tryphosa, dear. I know I'm several years older than you, but I'm not in the throes of dementia yet. *(Firmly)* You've *never* mentioned the name of Andrew Perryman in my presence...and if you *had* done, I'd have *remembered* it. So if you *want* to continue with what you were saying, you'd better start at the beginning then I'm not *completely* in the dark. *(Puts her cup on the coffee table)*

(TRYPHOSA gives a frustrated sigh and glares at her.)

TRYPHOSA. *(pointedly)* Do you remember me mentioning I was *adopted*?

MARIANNE. Of course I do. You've told me several times. Not that you needed to bother. I'd read your autobiography *long* before you came to Durning-on-Tace.

TRYPHOSA. *(nodding)* Then you also know that my real
mother dumped me on the Walburys' doorstep in
1943 and left me there to freeze to death.

MARIANNE. *(mildly)* A slight exaggeration, wouldn't you
say? I don't recall August being *that* cold. *(Kindly)*
But a dreadful thing to do, in any case. The poor girl
must have been desperate. *(Frowning)* And they never
discovered who she was, did they?

TRYPHOSA. *(waspishly)* I don't suppose anyone *tried.* I wasn't
the first unwanted child to end up in someone else's
care. And she never came back to see if I'd survived
the bombing...

MARIANNE. *(quietly)* Times were different then. In those
days unmarried mothers were stigmatized by all and
sundry. *(Wistfully)* Nowadays, it's almost a sign of
sainthood. *(Soothingly)* But she must have loved you,
whoever she was.

TRYPHOSA. *(surprised)* Why's that?

MARIANNE. The note she left pinned to the shawl you
were wrapped in. *(Quotes)* "Please take care of little
Tryphosa." If she hadn't loved you, why would she
have done that? *(Musing)* And such an unusual name.
Tryphosa. I'd never come across it, before.

TRYPHOSA. *(pointedly)* Which is what I'm trying to tell
you. I've found out where it came from. I was
watching television last week, and some...nobody...
on the programme was going on about tracing her
ancestry. *(Hastily)* Not that I'd the slightest interest,
you understand...until she mentioned she was trying
to find her grandmother's sister who'd left the family
home after the war ended...together with with her
baby girl, *Tryphosa.*

MARIANNE. *(surprised)* You're not...?

TRYPHOSA. *(dismissing the thought)* No, no, no. Of course
not. That was nineteen forty-six. *I* was born in forty-one.
She could hardly leave a five year old in a shopping
basket. And in any case, before the programme ended,

they told her they'd found Tryphosa's son…who'd been living in Dorking since nineteen sixty-eight…and introduced them to each other. *(Wrinkling her nose)* It was all very maudlin, as you can imagine, till someone had the sense to ask him where his mother got her name from.

MARIANNE. Well *I* could have told you that. I looked it up on Google. It's from the Bible.

TRYPHOSA. *(shaking her head)* A French opera singer in the early 1900s. Though she might have been German or Italian, he wasn't quite sure. *(Expanding on it)* I mean it's even possible she was American or Australian, because quite a few of them lived in France in those days. For the coaching, you understand. Matilde Marchesi was the best teacher in Paris and had pupils from all over the world. Melba, Calve'…

MARIANNE. *(firmly)* Tryphosa.

TRYPHOSA. *(protesting)* I was only *saying.* *(Continuing the narrative)* Well apparently, his paternal great-grandfather had been a devoted fan, and insisted his newly-born granddaughter be named after her. Daddy hated the whole idea, left the church after the christening, headed back to the US of A, where he hailed from, and was never heard of again. Momma Tryphosa died in two thousand and four.

MARIANNE. So how does this help you?

TRYPHOSA. *(glaring at her)* If you'll stop interrupting, I'll tell you.

(MARIANNE picks up her cup again.)

Not surprisingly, I always regarded Joan Walbury as my mother. Her sisters, Rhoda and Winifred, were my supposed aunts, of course…and before she married Lional Walbury, her maiden name was Greenwood. Now *that* didn't mean a thing. Not at the time. But last week Andrew found out that Grandmother Greenwood was a Malleson before she married, and that means

I'm a step nearer to finding out exactly who my real parents were.

MARIANNE. *(shaking her head)* Now you've *totally* lost me. If the Walburys adopted you, how on earth could tracing their ancestors, help you to find out who yours were?

TRYPHOSA. *(in disbelief)* It's perfectly obvious. *(With great emphasis)* George Malleson was the name of Ivor Kennedy's great-grandfather.

MARIANNE. *(baffled)* And who's Ivor Kennedy?

TRYPHOSA. *(exasperated)* The man on the television, of course. Tryphosa's *son*.

MARIANNE. *(heavily)* I think I need more tea. *(Begins to rise)*

TRYPHOSA. *(firmly)* Somehow or other, there's a connection between George Malleson and myself.

MARIANNE. *(moving towards the tea tray)* And how do you work that out? It could be pure coincidence.

TRYPHOSA. With a name like mine? How many Tryphosas do you know? You said so yourself. You'd never come across it before.

MARIANNE. *(reasonably)* I wasn't around at the start of last century, but if she happened to be in the public eye, it wouldn't surprise me that mothers named their daughters after her. *(Picks up the teapot)* Look at today. Half the world is named after pop singers, footballers or so-called celebrities.

TRYPHOSA. *(firmly)* Tryphosa Bates was an artiste. And besides…she couldn't have been that well known. She never appeared at Covent Garden or anywhere else in Britain. I've checked. So if someone named me after her, it must have been someone who'd heard her in the flesh…and George Malleson is the most likely suspect. He spent ten years in Paris, so they said. *(As the thought strikes her)* I could be her illegitimate daughter. It would explain the voice.

MARIANNE. That's very unlikely, dear. *(Pours a little tea then frowns as the pot appears to be empty)* Voices are rarely inherited, and if she was singing in Paris in the early nineteen-hundreds, she'd have been at least sixty by the time you were born.

TRYPHOSA. *(persisting)* Well her granddaughter then. It's possible. She could have left Paris to escape the Germans.

MARIANNE. And abandoned her baby on the Walbury's doorstep? Very operatic, dear. It's a wonder she didn't leave half a dozen scores for you to study during the Black-outs. *(Kindly)* I'm sorry, Tryphosa. but don't you think it's a little late to start wondering who your real parents were? The Walbury's gave you everything you wanted. You said so yourself. Just be happy they adopted you and didn't let you go to an orphanage.

TRYPHOSA. *(tartly)* It's not a case of being happy. It's all very well for you. You know who your family were. I want to know who mine were, too. And since Lewis, for some reason, left me most of his fortune when he died, I mean to find out. *(Frowns)* I still can't believe it. I hardly got a cent out of him when we divorced, and can't tell you what I went through, trying to pick up the pieces after moving to New York. God knows what I'd have done if darling Beverley hadn't been on the board of City Opera. She re-started my career and I'll not hear a word said against her. Sills was an angel to me. She adored my Zerbinetta.

MARIANNE. *(dryly)* I'm sure she did. But getting back to this research. What if you discover something you'd rather not have done? In my experience, it's always best to let sleeping dogs lie. Raking up the past can be dangerous.

TRYPHOSA. *(petulantly)* You wouldn't be saying that if you were trying to trace your real mother.

MARIANNE. *(nodding)* Maybe you're right. It's just that I don't see what difference it's going to make. Joan Walbury was the one who *raised* you. What does it matter who your birth mother was?

TRYPHOSA. It matters to *me*. I don't want to die not knowing where I came from. Surely I deserve that much?

MARIANNE. *(soothingly)* Of course you do. It's just that... well...it all sounds so vague. And what it must be costing to *hire* this man...

TRYPHOSA. Who cares about money? I've enough now to last twenty lifetimes. The only one who'll be concerned is darling Carla. And isn't she in for a shock? *(Smirking)* She'll not see a penny of it. I've made quite sure of that.

(**MARIANNE** *frowns.*)

MARIANNE. *(uneasily)* You've not cut her out of your *will?*

TRYPHOSA. *(airily)* She was never *in* it. *(Correcting herself)* Well...she was at one time. Before she decided to spit in my face and marry Harvey Gunter-Mason. *(Incredulously)* Can you believe it? Harvey Gunter-Mason. If it hadn't been for him, I'd have sung *Tosca* in Washington instead of that dreadful Castinella woman. *(Hastily)* Oh, she'd a good enough voice, but her acting was terrible. And the *figure*, my dear. Forty stone if she weighed an ounce. Could you imagine her flinging herself off the top of Castel Sant' Angelo? She'd have caused an earthquake when she hit the ground. *(Bitterly)* But she and Harvey were having an affair, and with him being their wealthiest supporter, the Board gave *me* the push and I ended up doing *Trovatore* with De Stefano in Philadelphia. Lovely voice, but my God, didn't he know it. I'd no idea, of course, my own daughter was another of Harvey's conquests, but the minute I found out, I'd no choice but to make a new will. She wasn't getting a penny of my money while she was living it up on his. *(Sagely)* Never trust Americans, Marianne. If they're patting you on the back, they're only looking for a soft spot to slide the knife in.

MARIANNE. *(dryly)* It didn't stop you marrying two of them.

TRYPHOSA. *(dismissively)* And both of them swines, darling. Joe was more interested in bedding his stable-boys than taking care of my needs, and *Lewis*...well...let's just say he made Don Giovanni look like a Vestal Virgin.

MARIANNE. *(pointedly)* According to your book, you weren't exactly Caesar's wife, yourself.

TRYPHOSA. *(waving this aside)* Pure invention. Just titivation to get the public salivating and increase sales. As a matter of fact, I was only unfaithful twice in my whole career. Once with the conductor of the Vienna Opera...and once with the Philadelphia orchestra.

(MARIANNE stares at her.)

It's a joke, Marianne. I never looked at another man during my time with Lewis. *(Correcting herself)* Well... I may have looked, but I was too busy building my reputation to do anything about it. *(Frowning)* I thought you were making fresh tea?

MARIANNE. *(glancing at the teapot)* If you ever stop talking and let me get on with it, I am. *(She turns to exit.)*

TRYPHOSA. Oh...and by the way. I won't be staying for dinner this time. I'm meeting Andrew in The Woltard Hotel at six. To hear what else he's found out.

MARIANNE. *(dryly)* In my opinion, it's that a fool and her money are soon parted.

(The door chimes sound.)

(Frowning) Now who's that?

*(She puts the teapot down and exits. **TRYPHOSA** picks up the magazine again and flicks through it distastefully. A moment later **MARIANNE**'s voice is heard.)*

(Off: surprised) Amy.

*(**TRYPHOSA** looks up and frowns.)*

AMY. *(off)* Sorry to trouble you, Mrs Grayson, but is Mother still here?

MARIANNE. *(off, warmly)* Come in. Come in.

(A moment later she enters the room.)

It's Amy.

(She steps aside right, to allow her to enter. **AMY BEVERAGE** *is a mousey, nervous woman of 45, in a plain pastel coloured dress and a long sleeved cardigan. She wears sensible flat shoes, and carries a small handbag containing a mobile phone. Her almost colourless face is marred by a black eye, which she has attempted to disguise without much success.)*

AMY. *(seeing* **TRYPHOSA***)* Mum. *(Moves down left of the sofa)*

TRYPHOSA. *(sharply)* Has he hit you again?

AMY. *(embarrassed)* Of course he hasn't, mother. I told you. He doesn't do that. I walked into a door.

TRYPHOSA. *(scornfully)* And last week you fell down the stairs. *(Harshly)* I'm not *stupid*, Amy. You've bruises all down your arms, and I suspect a cracked rib or two…

AMY. *(throwing a worried look at* **MARIANNE***)* Mother.

TRYPHOSA. Do you think I don't know what's going on? *(Firmly)* No one knows more about breathing than a singer. I can hear you're in pain from here.

AMY. *(protesting)* But I'm *not*. There's nothing wrong with me. It's just the cold I had last week. You know that. Frank wouldn't lay a finger on me.

TRYPHOSA. *(acidly)* Then what are you doing here?

AMY. *(patiently)* You had a call from your agent.

TRYPHOSA. *(frowning)* Donald? *(Dismissively)* He hasn't rung me in weeks. I thought he'd died. *(Impatiently)* What did he want?

AMY. Someone's been trying to get hold of you. From Heritage Research. A Mr Perryman.

TRYPHOSA. Andrew? Why would he ring my agent? He's had my mobile number for days.

AMY. *(pointedly)* You left it behind again. *(Fumbles in her bag for the phone)* I've brought it over.

(She finds it and offers it to **TRYPHOSA***.)*

TRYPHOSA. *(balefully)* Have you ever considered I might leave it behind because I *want* to? Unlike some people, my life does not revolve around mobile telephones and electronic devices. *(Takes the phone)* Given a choice between this and clean knickers, the latter would win hands down. *(Stuffs it in her pocket)*

AMY. *(soothingly)* He's been trying to reach you all morning. Mr Perryman, I mean.

TRYPHOSA. *(suddenly interested)* Why? Has he found something?

AMY. *(baffled)* I've no idea. He just asked if someone could let you know he can't make it tonight, after all, but he'll speak to you tomorrow if it's convenient.

TRYPHOSA. *(put out)* Damn. I was looking forward to having a decent meal for a change. Now I'll have to eat here again. *(Realising what she has said and speaking to* MARIANNE*)* No offence, darling, but you know how I love Italian food, and The Woltard do a wonderful *Tournedos Rossini.*

AMY. *(curious)* Are you writing another book, Mother?

TRYPHOSA. *(frowning)* Book?

AMY. *(awkwardly)* Heritage Research.

TRYPHOSA. *(sharply)* That's none of your business. You've done what you came to do, so Marianne can see you out again. I'll be home at the usual time. Providing I can find a driver who doesn't need a SatNav to find his way out of the taxi rank.

AMY. *(helpfully)* Frank could pick you up. He's coming home early today.

TRYPHOSA. *(acidly)* I'd sooner my chauffeur was a one-eyed camel driver with halitosis. *(Rises)* I need the bathroom, Marianne.

MARIANNE. *(resignedly)* You know where it is.

(Ignoring AMY, TRYPHOSA *sweeps past her and out of the room.)*

MARIANNE. *(to* **AMY**, *soothingly, moving right behind the sofa)*
Just ignore her, dear. She's been in a strange mood
since she arrived this morning. *(Moves down right of the
sofa)* Your sister, again, I expect.

AMY. *(surprised)* Carla? Why? What's she done *now?*

MARIANNE. *(shrugging)* I've no idea. But I thought it a
reasonable assumption. *(Sighs)* Though I never know
if your mother's serious when she goes on about her.
She makes the poor woman sound like some kind of
monster.

AMY. *(ruefully)* They *do* argue a lot. On the odd occasions
they're *speaking* to each other.

MARIANNE. *(wisely)* Then maybe it's as well that they live so
far apart. *(Smiles)* Can I offer you some tea before you
go? I was making fresh when you arrived.

AMY. *(uneasily)* It's very kind of you, but...

MARIANNE. It's no trouble. *(Indicates the armchair left)* Sit
yourself down.

*(**AMY** moves reluctantly to it.)*

Oh, just a moment. There's something on your cheek.
(Pulls out a clean handkerchief and crosses to her) Greenfly.
*(Dabs at **AMY**'s damaged cheek gently)* There. That's
better. Such a nuisance at this time of year. *(Puts the
handkerchief away)* I'm forever spraying my roses and
Lupins. *(Smiles)* A slice of fruit cake or a biscuit?

AMY. *(quickly)* Oh, no. Just tea will be fine. I mustn't be late
back. In case Carla comes round. *(She sits.)*

MARIANNE. *(puzzled)* Is she not staying with you, then?

AMY. *(shaking her head)* Oh, no. She wouldn't stay with us.
Not with Frank being there. *(Embarrassed)* They were
going to be married, at one time, you see?

MARIANNE. *(surprised)* Your husband and Carla?

AMY. *(nodding)* They met at Covent Garden. When Mother
was singing there. Carla went backstage after the
performance, and there he was. It was love at first
sight. They were laughing and joking by the stage

door while mother changed out of her costume and waited for her. *(Remembering)* There was an awful row afterwards. Mum had booked a table at Balmain's, and hated being late, but Carla said she'd have to go on her own because *she* was off to dinner with Frank and there was nothing Mum could do to stop her. Then she stormed off in a temper and didn't come home again for almost a week.

MARIANNE. *(intrigued)* And then what happened?

AMY. *(shrugging)* She and Frank got engaged. But six months later she dropped him like a hot brick and went to Italy without a word. We found out later she was living with a fashion designer in Rome. Quite rich, of course. She only had time for men with money. Why she threw herself at Frank, I can't imagine. He was only in the chorus and hadn't two ha'pennies to rub together...

MARIANNE. *(frowning)* I hadn't realised he sang.

AMY. *(adoringly)* Oh, yes. He had a lovely voice according to mother. She'd been paying for his lessons with a teacher in Hampstead till Carla sank her claws into him. But after she cancelled their agreement, he couldn't afford them himself.

MARIANNE. *(hesitantly)* So how did you and he...?

AMY. *(beaming)* Oh, I'd known him for almost as long as she did. He used to cry on my shoulder and ask what he'd done to make her leave him like that, and of course I visited him in hospital after his accident, so I suppose it was inevitable we'd get together after he came out. I mean...he was living with us till the day we got married.

MARIANNE. *(surprised)* And your mother was happy about this?

AMY. *(brightly)* Oh, yes. It was her idea in the first place. He couldn't go back to the place he'd been in. He needed looking after.

MARIANNE. *(puzzled)* But if she didn't like him...?

AMY. *(protesting)* But she did. She adored him. Everyone did. She was so furious about the way Carla had treated him, when we decided to marry, she offered to fund any further treatment to get him back on his feet again. But he said it would be a waste of time. When the voice is gone, there's nothing anyone can do about it.

MARIANNE. *(curious)* He lost his *voice?*

AMY. *(nodding)* There was a fight. In the street outside his flat. Two drunks were brawling and he tried to separate them. One of them stabbed him in the throat with a broken bottle and he couldn't speak for weeks. Afterwards it turned out his vocal chords had been affected worse than they thought, and his career was over. *(Hastily)* You'd never know, though. I mean…it was all years ago, and he speaks as well as you and I do, now. He just…can't sing any more.

MARIANNE. *(shocked)* She never told me that. *(Quickly)* Not that she'd any reason to, of course. But the poor man. *(As the thought strikes her)* Did Carla know what had happened to him?

AMY. Oh, yes. I wrote to her a few weeks before she left Guido and went to America, but she never replied. I know she got the letter, though, because she met Mother in Washington a few years later and mentioned it.

MARIANNE. And what about your father? Where was *he* when all this was going on?

AMY. He died when we were teenagers. It was Joe we were living with then. Her second husband. An American with a half-interest in a racing stable just outside London. *(Frowns)* I'm not sure what went wrong there, but we were whisked away to New York and never saw him again. By the time we came back to England, Mother was going through her third divorce, I'd left my job with Max Factor – I'd been learning make-up techniques – and had started working as her personal assistant.

MARIANNE. *(kindly)* I expect you miss it all now? The first nights and all that beautiful music.

AMY. Not really. It was exciting to meet the big names, etcetera, but I didn't appreciate the music. I'm tone deaf, you see? *(She smiles wanly.)* Can't tell my *Tosca* from my *Tales of Hoffman*...

MARIANNE. *(sympathetically)* Oh, you poor thing. I couldn't live without my music. I've been an opera lover since I was a girl. You've only to look at my collection... *(She waves her hand at the CD shelves)* I've always regretted your mother never recorded...though I've seen her on stage many times. *(Frowning)* Why none of the recording companies snapped her up, I can't imagine. I'll remember her *Turandot* till the day I die. She truly was a great singer.

*(*TRYPHOSA *re-enters, now wearing a matching light coat to her suit.)*

TRYPHOSA. Who was?

MARIANNE. *(turning to her)* You were. I was singing your praises. *(Frowns at the sight of the coat)*

TRYPHOSA. *(dryly)* Then you're fifteen years too late, dear. The last time I sang in public, the critics said I sounded like Callas on an off-day and should have retired before the curtain went up. *(Moves down left of the sofa)*

AMY. *(protesting)* No they didn't, Mother.

TRYPHOSA. *(frostily)* Don't contradict. And I thought you'd gone.

MARIANNE. I asked her to stay for tea.

TRYPHOSA. Good. It's saved me from chasing after her. But there's no time for tea, Marianne. As I'm not meeting Andrew now, I'm taking the opportunity to do something I *should* have done weeks ago. *(To* AMY*)* I've just spoken to my specialist, and he'll see us this afternoon. Are you wearing clean underwear?

AMY. *(startled)* What?

TRYPHOSA. You've obviously no intention of reporting your husband for assault, Amy, but I have no such reservation. You'll have a full examination, complete with photographs and x-rays, then everything will be given to my solicitor. *(To* **MARIANNE***)* I'll see you next week, dear. *(Moves upstage to exit)*

MARIANNE. *(hastily)* Your handbag. *(Picks it up and holds it out)*

AMY. *(rising)* I won't do it, Mother. I've told you again and again. Frank's got nothing to do with this. I'm just clumsy. You know that. *(Bitterly)* You've told me often enough.

TRYPHOSA. *(firmly)* Nevertheless, you'll see Dr Lorrimar and get this sorted out. I'll not stand by and watch you beaten to a pulp by an obvious psychopath.

AMY. *(hotly)* He's not a psychopath. And if anyone needs to see a doctor, it's you. You're not my keeper any more. I'm a married woman. You're just a… *(Struggles for words)* control freak.

TRYPHOSA. *(unperturbed)* Perhaps so. But one with more intelligence than to believe you damaged your eye by walking into a door. *(Scornfully)* I wasn't born yesterday, Amy. The man needs locking up.

(**AMY** *gives a sob and hurries out of the room.*)

(Calling after her sharply) Amy. *(Turning to* **MARIANNE** *and taking the handbag from her)* Sorry about that, Marianne. But I've got to do something. I may have failed with Carla, but it won't happen with Amy.

MARIANNE. *(uneasily)* It's none of my business, Tryphosa, but are you sure Frank's ill treating her? She could be just accident prone. You're always telling me…

TRYPHOSA. *(icily)* Do you think I don't know my own daughter? *(Softening)* I've suspected it for years. *(Grimly)* But he's not getting away with it. If Lorrimar confirms that she *is* being abused, I may not wait for the police to handle it. I'll kill him myself.

MARIANNE. Tryphosa…

TRYPHOSA. You don't know how lucky you are, Marianne. Only yourself to think about. No commitments. No husband. No family. I'd give my eye-teeth to be in your position.

MARIANNE. *(quietly)* It can have its down side.

TRYPHOSA. I can't think why it should. You're not short of money. You own a beautiful home and have friends to visit you. What more could you want?

MARIANNE. *(sighing)* I don't really know to be honest. I enjoy my music, and the garden, of course, but… well…there's sometimes too many hours in the day.

TRYPHOSA. *(in mock astonishment)* You have to be joking. I don't give a damn for *any* political party, but I'd vote for the BNP if they promised me a thirty-hour day. *(Firmly)* What *you* need, dear, is a hobby.

MARIANNE. *(amused)* I don't think so.

TRYPHOSA. *(firmly)* Of course you do. Oh, nothing stupid like stamp collecting, or trainspotting. Something that will occupy your mind. Painting…Brass Rubbing… *(Thinks rapidly)* Researching your Family Tree. Now there's an idea.

MARIANNE. *(apologetically)* I'm not really interested in researching…

TRYPHOSA. *(scornfully)* Of course you are. *Everyone's* interested in knowing who their ancestors were.

MARIANNE. I know all I want to know about my ancestors.

TRYPHOSA. *(insistently)* No you don't. You couldn't possibly. Where did your love of music come from, for instance? You did say your grandmother came from Germany, didn't you? So. You could be related to Mozart for all you know.

MARIANNE. That's *most* unlikely.

TRYPHOSA. Beethoven, then…or Offenbach…or a barrel organist from Bavaria. The point is, you never know *what* you're going to find out. Look at me. I didn't know anything about my family till last week. Now I'm about to find out my real mother's name. *(Firmly)* I'll have a word with Andrew tomorrow. He'll know *just* how to get you started.

MARIANNE. *(wearily)* Tryphosa. I'm not paying out good money—

TRYPHOSA. It'll be my treat. God knows I'm not going to miss a pound or so, and you're the only honest friend I've got. Give him a few weeks and you'll have ancestors pouring through the letterbox.

MARIANNE. *(protesting)* But I don't *want* them pouring through the letterbox. I'm perfectly happy as I am.

TRYPHOSA. You're saying that now, Marianne, but if you find out you're a direct descendant of Handel, you'll be singing a different song. Now don't keep me here any longer. God knows where she's gone to hide herself, but she's seeing Aiden Lorrimar this afternoon if I have to drag her there kicking and screaming. *(Heads for the arch again, then turns back)* Oh, and before I forget... I've got tickets for *Russalka* next Wednesday. I'll pick you up at six and we can have drinkies with Moretti before it begins. He's only conducting the first two performances, then he's off to Berlin for *Lucia*. *(Archly)* With a bit of luck, he might ask me to join him. *(Winks, then turns again and exits)*

MARIANNE. *(despairingly)* Tryphosa... *(Begins to follow her)*

TRYPHOSA. *(off)* Don't forget. Six o clock, sharp.

(The door slams, off, and **MARIANNE** *halts.)*

MARIANNE. *(peeved)* I don't *want* my family tree researched, and I've already bought my ticket for *Russalka*. *(Annoyed)* Why is it she never listens?

(She closes her eyes and stands for a moment before giving a deep sigh and shaking her head. Opening her eyes again, she moves to the coffee table and picks up the cups and saucers before moving out of the room. The lights slowly fade for the end of the scene.)

Scene Two

(Later that evening. Apart from the opera magazine, which has been replaced on the sofa, the room is unchanged. Outside, the light is fading, and **MARIANNE** *sits in the armchair right, half asleep, listening to a recording of "Vissi d'Arte" from Puccini's opera, "Tosca". After a moment, the door-chimes sound and she opens her eyes, disorientated. As the aria continues, the chimes sound again, and she levers herself to her feet, turns down the volume, then heads for the arch unsteadily and exits.)*

MARIANNE. *(off, uncertainly)* Who is it?

AMY. *(off, muffled)* It's Amy, Mrs Grayson. Amy Beverage.

(There is a short pause as **MARIANNE** *supposedly opens the door)*

(Clearer) We're so sorry to bother you, but could we have a word?

MARIANNE. *(off, uncertainly)* Of course, dear. Come in. Is something wrong? It's not your mother, is it?

AMY. *(off)* No, no. Wipe your feet, Frank. Well in a way it is, but it's nothing to worry about. She's not ill, or anything.

*(**MARIANNE** re-enters the room, followed by* **AMY**, *who is now dressed in a skirt, long-sleeved, high-necked blouse, and carrying a small handbag.* **FRANK BEVERAGE**, *her husband, is close behind.* **FRANK** *is in his early fifties and wears dark trousers, a white shirt and a summer jacket. He appears to be rather uncomfortable.)*

MARIANNE. *(relieved)* Thank goodness for that. When one gets to our age… *(Indicates the sofa)* Please. Take a seat. *(She moves to the music centre and turns it off)*

*(**AMY** and **FRANK** seat themselves.)*

AMY. *(anxiously)* You're sure we're not disturbing you? I know it's *late*.

MARIANNE. *(moving down right)* I'm never in bed before ten. And you're not disturbing me. I was just listening to an old recording.

FRANK. *Tosca.* Second act. I recognized it when you opened the door.

AMY. *(introducing him)* This is Frank. My husband. I've brought him along to tell you something. *(To* **FRANK***)* Haven't I, Frank? *(Nudging him)* Go on.

FRANK. *(awkwardly)* I know what you must be thinking of me, Mrs Grayson. After what Tryphosa said this morning. But it's not true. I've never laid a finger on Amy. She's got it all wrong.

MARIANNE. *(nonplussed)* Well... I'm glad to hear it. But... what's it to do with *me?*

AMY. *(earnestly)* You're her oldest friend, Mrs Grayson...her only friend, really. She's told me that, many a time. If she'll listen to anyone, it's you.

MARIANNE. *(still bewildered)* I don't understand.

AMY. *(embarrassed)* We had *another* argument this afternoon. and it turned into something of a screaming match. Poor Frank walked in just as she started her mad scene and caught the full brunt of it. To cut a long story short, she told him to get out and never come near the place again, and *I* said if Frank went, then I'd go with him.

MARIANNE. *(sympathetically)* Oh, dear. *(Sits in the chair right)* So what happened then?

FRANK. *(grimacing)* She stormed out like one of the Valkyries.

AMY. But not before telling us she was changing her will again. She said she'd make damn sure Frank never got his hands on her money...and neither would *I* until I came to my senses and divorced him.

MARIANNE. *(dismayed)* Oh, Amy, dear.

AMY. *(helplessly)* So that's why we've come to see *you.*

MARIANNE. *(puzzled)* But what can *I* do?

FRANK. We want you to tell her she's wrong about what she's imagined. I wouldn't hit Amy if my life depended on it. I love her, Mrs Grayson.

MARIANNE. I'm sure you do. But... *(Hesitates)* how can *I* help? You know what she's like. Once she gets an idea in her head, it's almost impossible to change it.

AMY. *(pleading)* But you don't *need* her money, Mrs Grayson, and we *do*. If she cuts me out of her will, we'll have *nothing*.

MARIANNE. *(surprised)* I don't think it'll come to that, dear. She won't leave you penniless when she finds out she's wrong. Tell her you will see this doctor of hers...if only to prove she's mistaken. She'll soon come to her senses.

AMY. *(unhappily)* But it's so degrading. Frank wouldn't hit me if someone paid him.

MARIANNE. Then seeing this doctor's the easiest way of proving it. *(Puzzled)* But what did you mean by saying *I* didn't need her money? She's not leaving me something, is she?

AMY. *(awkwardly)* You'll be her main beneficiary.

(MARIANNE stares at her in shock.)

MARIANNE. *(confused)* There must be some mistake. I don't want her money. I've investments of my own...and *more* than enough for my lifetime.

AMY. *(shaking her head)* I read the draft of her new will myself. Just before we came here. She left it on the desk. *(Hastily)* I wasn't snooping, or anything. I've *always* checked her letters and things before she finalized them. She's asked me to. To save embarrassment.

FRANK. *(explaining)* Tryphosa's dyslexic, you see? Not many people know, but for some reason, she feels it's something to be ashamed of, which is absolute rubbish. *(Wryly)* It's how I came to meet her. It slipped out in rehearsals one day, and she asked me for help. If I'd go through any new roles with her, she'd pay for my coaching lessons. I couldn't believe my luck and jumped at the offer. Who wouldn't?

AMY. I'd been helping her deal with it for years, but I could only do it when I wasn't at university.

FRANK. If it hadn't been for Amy, *Darling of the Gods* might never have been published.

MARIANNE. *(fretfully)* But why does she want to leave *me* anything? A small memento, I could understand. That lovely brooch she sometimes wears, for instance. She knows I admire that. But what you're suggesting…

AMY. About fifty-six million. After taxes and the *other* bequests are deducted.

(MARIANNE's mouth opens as if to speak, then her eyes roll and she sags into the chair.)

(Alarmed) Mrs Grayson…

FRANK. *(springing up)* Get some water. Quick. *(Hurries across and kneels beside her)*

(AMY hurries out of the room)

Mrs Grayson? Mrs *Grayson*? Can you hear me?

MARIANNE. *(weakly)* She mustn't do it. *(Her hand grips his arm and she attempts to sit up.)* I have to speak to her. Tell her she mustn't.

FRANK. You can tell her later. When you're feeling better.

MARIANNE. *(dazedly)* I never realized.

FRANK. Of course you didn't. No reason why you should. Even Amy's no idea how much her mother's actually worth. Most of it's in Swiss banks, where this government can't get its hands on it.

(AMY hurries in with a glass of water and crosses to them.)

AMY. What is?

FRANK. *(holding out his hand for the glass)* Your mother's money.

AMY. *(giving it to him)* Oh. *(To MARIANNE)* Are you feeling better?

(**FRANK** *assists* **MARIANNE** *with the glass.*)

You went such a funny colour.

MARIANNE. *(after a sip of water)* I'm fine, thank you. Fine. *(Takes another sip)*

FRANK. Would you like me to call someone?

MARIANNE. *(shakily)* No, no. It was just the shock. I'm alright now. Really, I am. *(Sips the water again)*

AMY. *(distressed)* I *knew* I shouldn't have said anything. The minute I opened my mouth. She told me you had a weak heart. I'm so sorry.

MARIANNE. *(shaking her head, carefully)* It wasn't your fault, dear. No need to upset yourself. *(More firmly)* But we have to do something to make her change her mind. I couldn't possibly allow her to leave me all that money. If anyone should have it, it's you and your sister. Not an old woman who's already got more than she knows what to do with.

AMY. *(unhappily)* Which is why we came round to see you. It's her money, of course, but how are we going to live if she does cut me out of her will? We won't have a penny to our name.

FRANK. *(rising and backing away to the sofa end)* Except for my income, such as it is, which wouldn't even buy us a two bedroomed flat.

AMY. She pays for everything, you see? Always has done. There isn't a thing we can call our own. And I doubt I'd find a job in this day and age. *(Bitterly)* Once you're past forty, you may as well be dead.

MARIANNE. *(forcing a smile)* I know how you feel, dear. If I hadn't married Gerald… *(Struggles for normality)* I'm sorry to have taken your news so badly. I never imagined. I mean… I knew she was wealthy, of course, *(Wryly)* but I've always taken her stories with a pinch of salt. She does tend to exaggerate. *(Firmly)* But you were certainly right to come here. If there's anything I can do, then rest assured I'll do it. *(She begins to rise)* I'll make us a cup of tea, shall I?

AMY. *(hastily)* No, no. You stay there. I'll do it.

MARIANNE. *(standing)* It's *my* house and you're *my* guests. It won't take more than a few minutes and it'll give me time to clear my mind. *(Taking the glass with her, she moves unsteadily up to the arch and exits.)*

(AMY *moves closer to* **FRANK.)**

AMY. *(anxiously and in a low voice)* Do you think we've done the right thing?

(FRANK*'s character changes to a much harder and threatening one.)*

FRANK. We'll find out when we see what happens. *(Scowling)* But you needn't have opened your mouth about how much she'd be getting. How many times have I told you? All folks need to know is what you want 'em to know. Treat 'em like mushrooms. Keep 'em in the dark and feed 'em horse manure.

AMY. *(timidly)* I'm sorry, Frank. It just slipped out.

FRANK. *(sneering)* Yes. Like it just "slipped out" when Mummy dearest started making her crazy accusations. She's as mad as a bloody hatter. *(Throws a quick glance at the arch)* Are you sure the old girl can stop her from changing the will? She seems ga-ga to me.

AMY. I told you. They've known each other for years. If anyone can do it, it's her.

FRANK. *(glowering)* You'd better be right, then. *(Sits on the sofa scowling)* But I still can't see why *she (He indicates the arch with his head)* should inherit anything. If anyone's entitled, it's us. Why should she be looked after while we're left to starve in the gutter?

AMY. It won't happen. Not now she's going to help. And if I do see Dr Lorrimar, Mother'll back down. I *know* she will.

FRANK. *(scowling)* And what if he says I've been slapping you around?

AMY. *(firmly)* I'll deny it. The way I always do. He can't prove anything.

FRANK. And what about Carla? You think she won't stick her nose in?

AMY. *(puzzled)* Why should she? She already knows she's not getting a cent of mother's money. Marrying Harvey put an end to that.

FRANK. *(coldly)* So what's she doing back here?

AMY. How should I know? It could be nothing more than a shopping trip.

FRANK. *(incredulously)* In Durning? *(Sneering)* You don't fly the Atlantic to shop in backwaters like this. A bitch like her would be living it up at the Savoy and spending her money in Harrods. *(Darkly)* No. She's up to something. And I want to know what it *is* before she gets a chance to interfere. Like I've always said... Keep one step in front, and there's no chance of nasty surprises.

*(**MARIANNE** re-enters, carrying a small tray containing tea things.)*

MARIANNE. *(beaming)* Here we are. *(Deposits the tray on the table behind the sofa.)*

AMY. *(rising)* Would you like me to help?

MARIANNE. No, no. I can manage. Both milk and sugar, is it?

FRANK. *(back to "charm")* Just the milk, please. Have to watch our waistlines. *(Laughs)*

*(As **AMY** sits again, **MARIANNE** pours milk into the cups, then begins pouring tea.)*

MARIANNE. Now then...before we go any further, I think I can put your minds at rest. As far as I can make out, if Tryphosa does cut you out of her will, it's most unlikely you'll be left penniless. You can appeal, you see? If she's been supporting you financially up to the time of her death, then she's morally bound to make provision for you, and a court would almost certainly rule in your favour. *(Proudly)* I looked it up while waiting for the kettle to boil. *(Hands a cup to* **AMY**.*)* Of course, you'd have to confirm it with your solicitor. I don't entirely believe *everything* I read on the internet. *(She picks up another cup)*

AMY. *(wincing)* We haven't got one, to be honest. Mother didn't believe in them. Said she'd had enough of solicitors dipping their paws into her finances, and was perfectly capable of writing her own legal documents.

FRANK. And we were hoping it wouldn't come to that. You know? Solicitors and things.

MARIANNE. *(reassuringly)* I'm sure it won't, Mr Beverage. *(Hands the cup to* FRANK*)* But it's something to remember if it should. *(Ruefully)* You know how stubborn she is? *(Picks up her own cup, adds sugar, stirs it and moves right to sit in the armchair)* However...I did have another thought. *(Sips at her tea)* All that money you spoke about. Fifty something million, didn't you say?

*(*AMY *nods.)*

(Shaking her head sadly) Well I couldn't cope with that. Really I couldn't. I know it'll sound silly to youngsters like you, but even the thought of having that much money worries the life out of me. I wouldn't know what to do with it, and I couldn't sleep at nights knowing she'd left it to me instead of her own daughters. So I hope you'll agree with what I'm about to suggest.

(She pauses and they look at her expectantly)

I'm not supposed to know about it, am I? The will, I mean.

AMY. *(shaking her head, ruefully)* I shouldn't have let it slip.

MARIANNE. *(understandingly)* So a straightforward approach would be quite the wrong thing.

FRANK. *(agreeing)* It *would* make it awkward. The mood she's in now.

MARIANNE. So if she's determined to change her will, we need a way to make her think again. And I think I have the answer. *(Smiles)*

AMY. *(hopefully)* What is it?

MARIANNE. *(triumphantly)* I'll tell her I'm re-writing my own will and leaving everything to you and Carla.

(They look at her in bewilderment.)

(Quickly) Oh, it'll be nothing compared to your mother's fortune, of course. Just the house and a few stocks and shares. But enough to keep you in comfort if you don't go *too* mad.

AMY. *(protesting)* No, no. You *can't*. We're not expecting—

MARIANNE. *(beaming)* I know, dear. But as your mother's well aware, I've no family left, and everything was going to Charity, anyway, so why not leave it to you and your sister instead?

AMY. *(protesting)* But you hardly know us. You've never even met Carla.

MARIANNE. Which will show your mother I don't agree with what she's proposing to do, and may make her think twice about changing her own will.

FRANK. *(puzzled)* I don't understand.

MARIANNE. It's quite simple. If she does change it…and providing she dies first…which I don't suppose will happen as I'm the elder by several years and much more likely to be pushing up daisies before she takes her final call… Amy and Carla will have everything of mine to look forward to, including whatever Tryphosa considers leaving me. *(Brightly)* If she thinks they'll still get her money if I inherit, then hopefully she'll leave things as they are.

FRANK. *(brightening)* You're right. Especially if Dr Lorrimar can convince her I'm not a wife beater. *(Grins widely at* MARIANNE*)*

AMY. *(unconvinced)* And what if he *can't*…? And *(gives an unhappy glance at* MARIANNE*)* Mrs Grayson dies first? Or finds out that she's been cut out of the will, too?

MARIANNE. *(firmly)* Then you'd share what I'm going to leave you, and appeal to the court when your mother dies. It's as simple as that. Now drink your tea or it'll be stone cold. *(Sips at her own cup)*

AMY. *(embarrassed)* I don't know what to say.

MARIANNE. *(kindly)* Then don't say *anything*. If everything goes to plan, you'll have nothing more to worry about and everything will sort itself out. I'll see my solicitor tomorrow.

(AMY and FRANK exchange glances.)

FRANK. *(oozing sincerity)* We don't know how to *thank* you, Mrs Grayson. We've no idea where Tryphosa got this idiotic impression I was ill-treating Amy from. We've been living with her for the last twenty years, and she can *see* how much we're in love. *(Frowns)* But she's acting so strangely these days. And drinking far more than she used to do. We're starting to wonder if she mightn't be…well…developing some kind of *dementia*.

MARIANNE. *(frowning)* I can't say *I've* noticed anything.

FRANK. *(hastily)* It's not all the time. Just the odd moments. Mainly in the evenings. She seems to lose track of things. Forget what she's talking about… or what she's been doing.

MARIANNE. *(amused)* In that case, you could say I'm heading in the same direction. There're days I'd forget my head if it wasn't attached to my body. The times I've stood at the bottom of the stairs wondering if I was going up or had just come down. No, no. There's nothing wrong with Tryphosa but good old-fashioned frustration.

(AMY looks puzzled.)

I'm surprised you've not noticed it yourself. How long is it since she retired? Sixteen years?

AMY. *(slowly)* About that. Yes.

MARIANNE. And what has she done since? Nothing. She's too impatient to teach, refuses to give talks or sit on the board at Covent Garden or La Scala, and hasn't read a book in years. It's no *wonder* she's looking round for something to sharpen her tongue on. One minute she's a superstar with the world at her feet, and the next, just an old lady like me with too much time on her hands and a head full of memories.

FRANK. But why pick on us?

MARIANNE. *(gently)* Because you're closest, of course. One's always harder on the ones you love. *(Wistfully)* I remember Barbara, many years ago. *(Drifts into a trance)*

AMY. *(after a moment)* Your sister?

MARIANNE. *(snapping out of it)* What? *(Remembering)* Oh, no. No. Barbara wasn't my *sister.* I was an only child. *(Smiles)* She was a cousin. A distant cousin. I used to stay with them during the summer holidays. Such a wonderful artist, even at eighteen. Most of the pictures in here *(indicates the room)* are hers. *(Dreamily)* One of the local boys was madly in love with her, but couldn't do anything right in her eyes, so it seemed. *(Shaking her head)* What a minx she was. I knew for a fact that she'd loved him since the day they met, but she teased and tormented him till the poor man was half out of his mind. *(Sadly)* And finally he killed himself. Said he couldn't live without her, and never found out how much she did care for him.

AMY. *(shocked)* How awful.

MARIANNE. She never got over the shock. A few days after the funeral, she left the village and vanished. Even her parents had no idea where she'd gone, and it was years after they'd died before the mystery was solved.

AMY. *(apprehensively)* She'd not killed herself?

MARIANNE. *(laughs)* Good gracious, no. She'd been living on a farm in Cornwall for the past twenty years or so...with a husband and two stepchildren. Well, I *say* husband...but they never actually married. Just lived together. Which was why she couldn't be traced, I suppose. They were looking for Barbara Freeman, not Barbara Tregorran.

FRANK. So…who found her, in the end? *(Deposits his cup on the coffee table)*

MARIANNE. No one. It only came out when she sent me a letter. Though by *that* time it was much too late. Her parents were long dead, as were my own, but she wanted someone to know she was safe and well, and I must have seemed the obvious choice. *(Sighs)* I can't tell you how *furious* I was. I really thought something terrible had happened to her. Not a word for almost thirty years, and suddenly she'd decided to put me out of my misery. *(Guiltily)* I said some very unkind things in my reply, so she phoned me, and begged me to visit and let her explain why she'd done what she had done. The boys had left home, gone to Canada or somewhere, and she and Tony had separated, so we'd be quite alone. *(Closes her eyes and falls silent)*

AMY. *(prompting)* And did you go?

MARIANNE. *(shakes her head)* I told her I'd think about it and put the phone down. *(Softly)* Two nights later, she was dead. According to the police, she'd been drinking heavily, fallen down stairs holding an oil lamp, and burned to death.

FRANK. *(frowning)* Oil lamp?

MARIANNE. *(sighs)* There was no electricity or gas, and even the water came from a well behind the house. The farm was too far from the mains, so they said, and a battery radio was her only concession to modern life. Even the nearest phone-box was over a mile away. I always blamed myself, of course. If I'd been more sympathetic and agreed to meet her, it might never have happened. But I was so *hurt.*

AMY. *(nodding)* Of course.

MARIANNE. Which is why I say "You're always harder on the ones you love." Anyone *else* I might have listened to, but Barbara… *(Sighs again)* Well… I think I expected too much of her. And that's the way your mother is,

Amy. She wants everything to be perfect. *(Sips at her tea and grimaces)*

FRANK. *(protesting)* But it *was*, Mrs Grayson. Till she got this weird idea into her head. If only we can sort this out, we'll be as happy as pigs in sh— *(corrects himself)* a trough of acorns.

MARIANNE. I'm sure you will, dear. *(Firmly)* I'll give her a call tomorrow and tell her what I'm going to do. I'm sure it'll give her pause. *(Struggling to her feet)* But let me make you some fresh tea. We've been chattering away so long it's practically cold. You haven't even *touched* yours.

AMY. *(putting her cup down as she rises)* We have to be going, actually. He's got an early start, tomorrow. *(To FRANK)* Haven't you, Frank? *(To MARIANNE)* But we don't know *how* to thank you. Not just for what you're doing, but... well...for everything.

(She quickly hugs MARIANNE, almost causing the tea to spill. FRANK stands.)

FRANK. You'll never know how grateful we are.

MARIANNE. *(chiding)* Now stop it, the pair of you. You're embarrassing me. If I can't help my dearest friend's children, I don't deserve to be called her friend. Just keep your fingers crossed I can persuade her to leave her multi-millions where they are. Can you imagine the fuss if I *can't*? The press'd have a field day. Tryphosa Swan's fortune going to someone like *me*, instead of her own family. I'd never live it down.

AMY. *(warmly)* You'd deserve every penny of it. *(To FRANK)* Wouldn't she, Frank?

FRANK. Without a doubt.

MARIANNE. *(hopefully)* Are you *sure* you wouldn't like more tea?

FRANK. *(shaking his head)* We'd better be off. I want to be through the town centre before the pubs turn out. You know what it's like mid-week. A close encounter of the yob kind isn't my favourite occupation, and tomorrow's a long day for me. But we'll never forget you for this, Mrs Grayson. Not for as long as we live. *(Awkwardly)* Would you mind if I used your loo?

MARIANNE. Of course not. It's the first on the right at the top of the stairs.

(**FRANK** *smiles his thanks and exits through the arch.*)

(To **AMY***)* He seems a nice man.

AMY. *(gushing)* Oh, he *is,* Mrs Grayson. I couldn't have picked better. He waits on me hand and foot. *(Coyly)* It's quite embarrassing sometimes.

MARIANNE. I know what you mean, dear. My Gerald was exactly the same. Treated me like bone china from the first day we met. *(Smiles)* Drove me mad at times. Wouldn't *dream* of letting me go to the opera on my own, for instance, and insisted on taking me though he hated every note and preferred Alma Cogan to Sylvia Fisher. Half the time, he was fast asleep before the overture ended. *(Lightly)* But then again, if it hadn't been for *him,* I might never have heard your mother sing. He bought tickets for my birthday, and I saw her in *Norma.*

AMY. *(frowning)* Really? But she never sang *Norma* in this country.

MARIANNE. *(smiling)* It was in Rome. We were there on holiday. And after that, I'm afraid I was hooked. Every time she sang in this country, I was there in the front stalls. And at the stage door afterwards. *(Smiles)* She must have thought I was mad, but I couldn't get enough of her. I wrote letter after letter to the record companies, begging them to record her, but all I got were polite replies. So in the end I wrote to her, and that's how our friendship started. You could have knocked me down with a feather when she sent me two tickets for *Daughter of the Regiment* and invited us backstage afterwards.

AMY. *(surprised)* I don't remember meeting you...

MARIANNE. *(shaking her head regretfully)* Gerald died. Two days before the performance. I returned the tickets, of course, and she sent a *beautiful* wreath. It was totally unexpected, and I'll never forget it. *(Fondly)* Such kindness from someone I hardly knew.

AMY. *(quietly)* Yes. She was always full of surprises.

MARIANNE. I couldn't believe it when she retired to this part of the world and bought the house in Huxton. It belonged to Sir Richard Oxley at one time. The conductor.

AMY. *(nodding)* That was the attraction, I think. She'd worked with him several times in her younger days and living in his old home seemed the perfect way to keep his memory alive. She was devastated when he died.

FRANK. *(re-entering)* Who's that?

AMY. *(turning to him)* Sir Richard Oxley.

FRANK. Oh. *(Remains left)*

MARIANNE. *(beaming)* I couldn't *wait* to let her know I only lived down the road, and the next morning she dropped in to say hello, stayed for the rest of the day, and we've been friends ever since.

FRANK. *(lightly)* You must have caught her on a good day. I've known her over thirty years and it's like living on a knife edge, sometimes.

AMY. *(chiding)* Frank.

MARIANNE. You have to know how to handle her. *(Confidentially)* I got *my* experience in dealing with difficult customers in the nursing home. Treat them with respect, but don't let them bully you. *(Eyes twinkling)* I expect I get away with far more than you two can. She's never turned her famous temper on *me*.

FRANK. *(lightly)* You don't know how lucky you are. Well, we'd better be off. And thank you again. For everything. You don't know how much we owe you.

MARIANNE. *(lightly)* I'll send you a bill if it all works out.

(They all move out through the arch and vanish from view.)

(Off) Watch how you go. And keep your fingers crossed.

AMY. *(off)* We will. We will. Bye.

FRANK. *(off)* Bye.

(A moment later, MARIANNE re-enters and begins to gather the discarded cups, placing them on the tray again. She then moves to the windows to close the drapes, but as she does so, she sneezes. Fishing out her handkerchief, she wipes her nose, and about to replace the handkerchief, looks at it with a frown. The door chime sounds. MARIANNE glances at her wrist-watch and stuffs the handkerchief back in her pocket before exiting through the arch.)

MARIANNE. *(off; warmly)* Come in, dear. Come in. They've just this minute left.

CARLA. *(off)* I know. I was watching from the car.

(MARIANNE re-enters followed by CARLA GUNTER-MASON, an elegantly dressed, though severe looking woman of fifty, wearing a summer top-coat and carrying an American style handbag under her arm.)

MARIANNE. *(Crossing right, behind the sofa, beaming)* It's so lovely to *see* you again.

CARLA. You, too. I can't *believe* how time's flown. *(Puts her purse down and unfastens her coat)*

MARIANNE. *(Fussily)* Is there anything I can get you? A cup of tea? Or something *stronger?*

CARLA. *(Removing her coat and draping it on the sofa back)* I'm fine, thank you. I just need a few words before I make my move. *(Moves round the sofa and sits)* Make sure there'll be no *mistakes.*

MARIANNE. *(Uneasily)* You're quite *determined,* then? You're really going to *do* it?

CARLA. *(Smiling coldly)* Oh, *yes.* From now on, bitchy little *Carla's* in the driving seat. *(Glowering)* And I don't intend using the *brakes.*

(MARIANNE sits in the armchair right as the lights fade and the curtains close for the end of the scene.)

Scene Three

(Late morning, two days later.)

(Once again, it is a fine day and apart from the curtains being open, CARLA's coat and the tea things removed, the room is unchanged and unoccupied. After a moment, the door chimes sound. There is a pause, then it sounds again. A moment or two later, TRYPHOSA's voice is heard off left.)

TRYPHOSA. *(off)* Are you there, Marianne?

(TRYPHOSA appears in the arch, now in a light trouser suit and blouse. She carries a matching and well stuffed handbag.)

Anyone home? *(Looks off to her left)* You'd better come in while I check upstairs.

ANDREW. *(off)* Are you sure it's all right?

TRYPHOSA. *(surprised)* Why shouldn't it be? We're not going to burgle the place.

ANDREW. *(off)* It's just...

TRYPHOSA. I told you this morning. Marianne's my dearest friend, and we always keep an eye out for each other.

(ANDREW PERRYMAN appears in the arch. He is in his thirties, spectacled and studious looking, and is dressed in dark trousers, light green shirt with an open neck, and a summer jacket. He carries an attaché case.)

That's why she gave me a key. If anything happened to her, at least there'd be no need to break the door down to get inside. *(Indicates the room)* Just find yourself a seat while I see if she's alright.

(She moves behind him and vanishes left.)

(Calling; off) Are you there, Mariannne? I've brought Mr Perryman to see you...

(ANDREW moves into the room, moving right, behind the sofa and glancing around with interest. After a slight hesitation, he sits in the chair right, still clutching the

attaché case. Noticing a mark on his trouser leg, he rubs at it gently, then fumbles in his jacket pocket for his handkerchief, extracts it, spits on it lightly and scrubs at the mark. Examining the result, he grimaces and replaces the handkerchief in his pocket. **TRYPHOSA** *re-enters the room.)*

(Briskly) Must be out. *(Moves down left)* Not a sign of her upstairs, and you can see right down the garden from her bedroom window.

(ANDREW *begins to rise.)*

No, no. Stay where you are. We'll wait till she's back. *(Sits on the sofa)* There's no hurry. *(Deposits her bag beside her)*

ANDREW. *(uncomfortable)* I *do* have another appointment, Ms Swan.

TRYPHOSA. *(unconcerned)* At a quarter past three. You mentioned it earlier. But there's nothing to worry about. She'll be back *long* before then. Tell me some more about the Malleson man.

ANDREW. *(frowns)* George Malleson, you mean? *(Shrugs)* There's nothing more to tell. I gave you everything I turned up on him the last time we spoke.

TRYPHOSA. *(disappointed)* But it doesn't *prove* anything, does it? Born in 1879, married a French dancer in 1902 and worked as a carpenter. You haven't even mentioned his time in Paris.

ANDREW. *(patiently)* Because there's nothing in the records to show that he *was* in Paris. At the moment, I've only your word for that.

TRYPHOSA. And his great-grandson's. Ivor Kennedy. Didn't you ask *him* about it?

ANDREW. *(wearily)* I haven't had the chance. The programme you saw last week was taped the week before, and by the time I found out where to find him, he and his family had gone off on holiday. They won't be back until the twenty-seventh.

TRYPHOSA. *(put out)* Well you can take my word for it. Ten years in Paris is what he said George Malleson did. Which is where he met Sabine.

ANDREW. Mr Kennedy's great-grandmother. Yes.

TRYPHOSA. *(light suddenly dawning)* At the Opera House.

ANDREW. *(frowning)* I'm sorry?

TRYPHOSA. *(rising excitedly)* I should have thought of it *before. (Moves down left)* Where *else* would a dancer meet a carpenter? *(Triumphantly facing him)* At the Opera House in Paris, of course…where he could have heard Tryphosa Bates sing.

ANDREW. *(reluctantly)* We can only assume that, Ms Swan.

TRYPHOSA. Of course we can't. *(Moves up left, working it out)* He marries Sabine in Paris… *(Snidely)*…probably *had* to, if I know French dancers. Comes back to England where his granddaughter marries an American who eventually dumps her because he hates his daughter's name. What more proof do we need?

ANDREW. *(tiredly)* Quite a lot, Ms Swan. We're looking for *your* ancestors, not Mr Kennedy's.

TRYPHOSA. *(moving right, behind the sofa: agitatedly)* But they're one and the same thing. You told me last week. Grandmother Greenwood was a Malleson before she married. She was probably George Malleson's sister.

ANDREW. He didn't *have* a sister. I've already checked. He was one of four boys.

TRYPHOSA. His daughter then. Or a niece. There must have been *some* connection.

ANDREW. *(mildly)* I'm sorry, Ms Swan. But up to now, there doesn't appear to be any link between George Malleson and your adoptive mother's mother.

TRYPHOSA. *(snappishly)* Then perhaps you're not looking hard enough. If you put more effort into what I'm paying you for, we might get better results.

ANDREW. *(stiffly)* If you're not satisfied… *(Beginning to rise)*

TRYPHOSA. *(hastily)* No, no. Just ignore me. *(Motions him to sit again)* Of course you're doing your best. It's just I'm so frustrated. *(Moves left, behind the sofa)* I *know* George Malleson knew my real mother. I'm convinced of it. All you need to do is find the connection.

ANDREW. *(sitting again)* Believe me, I'm trying to. But it's not always as simple as it appears to be on television. We know Sabine died in 1937, but there isn't a clue in The Family Records Centre as to when he died. All that *is* known, is what I've told you, and after his granddaughter's christening, he simply vanishes. Until I can speak with her son, we've no idea what happened to him, or where he went.

TRYPHOSA. *(moving down left)* Couldn't he have gone to France again?

ANDREW. It's possible. But 1946 or thereabouts? He'd be almost seventy.

TRYPHOSA. *(icily)* Is that some kind of problem?

ANDREW. *(hastily)* Of course not. I just mean the war was over, and providing he was still in good health, he could have gone *anywhere*. Canada. The USA...or even Australia. They were all options at the time.

TRYPHOSA. Could you check the shipping records?

ANDREW. Of course. But it may take some time. And it could be a wild goose chase. As I said earlier, there's no indication that Mr Malleson had anything to do with your adoptive family. *(Hastily)* But I'll keep on searching, I promise you.

TRYPHOSA. And what about Marianne?

ANDREW. *(shrugging)* Well... Apart from the anomaly I mentioned earlier, I don't see any problem. You *did* say her grandparents were German?

TRYPHOSA. Grand*mother*. She's never mentioned her grandfather.

ANDREW. Well... I can get Becky – my assistant – to dig into that. She's German born herself and...

TRYPHOSA. *(sharply)* No, Andrew. *(Moves right, towards him)* I want *you* to do it, personally. She's my dearest friend and I won't have anything second best for her. Do I make myself clear?

ANDREW. I'd hardly call anything Becky does second best. What *she* doesn't know about heritage research, isn't worth knowing. But if that's what you want…?

*(**MARIANNE**'s voice is heard off.)*

MARIANNE. *(brightly)* …Though it's hardly worth the bother, these days. It was much easier then. I'll put the kettle on, shall I?

*(**ANDREW** rises, looking towards the arch.)*

CARLA. *(off)* I can do that.

*(**TRYPHOSA** stares at the arch in disbelief.)*

MARIANNE. *(off)* No, no. You go in. I can manage.

*(She appears in the arch, wearing a flowery summer dress and carrying a shopping basket filled with paper bags of assorted goods. She sees **ANDREW** and **TRYPHOSA**.)*

(Startled) Tryphosa.

*(**CARLA** appears beside her, in a smart two-piece suit, and is also carrying a well-filled shopping bag.)*

TRYPHOSA. *(harshly, to **MARIANNE**)* What's *she* doing here?

CARLA. *(coolly)* What does it look like, Mother? I'm giving a hand with the groceries.

TRYPHOSA. *(snappishly)* I wasn't addressing *you.*

CARLA. *(unconcernedly)* When were you ever? *(Pretending to remember)* Oh, yes. I think we did have a conversation once. *(Bitterly)* About twenty years ago. Prior to that, it was mainly orders, if I remember right.

MARIANNE. Tryphosa…

TRYPHOSA. *(ignoring her)* You always did have a tongue like a viper.

CARLA. *(moving into the room)* And who did I inherit that from, I wonder? It certainly wasn't Father. He at least treated me as though I were human.

*(**ANDREW** looks very uncomfortable.)*

TRYPHOSA. *(bitterly)* And what a mistake that was. I should have smothered you at birth. *(Turns away and moves right)*

CARLA. *(amused)* Well you certainly never *mothered* me, that's for sure. I was eight years old before I found out who you were.

TRYPHOSA. *(turning to face her her, stung)* In case it's escaped your memory, I had a career.

CARLA. *(snapping back)* And I had a child-minder instead of a mother.

MARIANNE. *(distressed, but firmly)* Now that's *enough.* The pair of you. If you want to air your grievances, please find somewhere else to do it. I won't have it in *my* house.

TRYPHOSA. *(unexpectedly)* You're absolutely *right,* Marianne. I've wasted too many years attempting to reason with her. What's the point of arguing? She never listens. *(Narrowing her eyes)* But what I would like to know, is how you came to make her acquaintance? I didn't think you'd had the pleasure. *(Sourly)* For want of a better word.

*(**MARIANNE** opens her mouth to reply, but **CARLA** speaks first.)*

CARLA. *(dryly)* We met two years ago. When you were in hospital.

TRYPHOSA. *(surprised)* In England?

CARLA. *(flatly)* We may have our differences, but you're still my mother. I came the minute I heard.

TRYPHOSA. *(tightly)* From who?

CARLA. It was in the *New York Times.* I took the first flight from Kennedy and was here the next morning.

MARIANNE. She introduced herself in Reception. While we were waiting for news.

TRYPHOSA. *(Icily)* And you somehow forgot to mention it.

CARLA. I asked her not to. If it really had been a stroke, I didn't want you having another.

TRYPHOSA. *(snapping)* What do you mean, "If it had been a stroke"? I almost died.

CARLA. *(irritated)* It was unconfirmed, according to the doctor *I* spoke to. And if you hadn't made such a *drama* out of it, you'd have been home within the week.

TRYPHOSA. *(harshly)* I've been on Warfarin ever since.

CARLA. *(unconcerned)* I'm sure you have. Not to mention the fifty thousand other pills and potions you've been throwing down your throat for the past forty years. *(Glances at* **ANDREW***)* And I presume this pretty young man stays close at hand to make sure you take them all on time?

TRYPHOSA. *(acidly)* This pretty young man, as you call him, happens to be from Heritage Research. And he's here to see Mrs Grayson.

MARIANNE. *(realising)* Mr Perryman.

CARLA. *(to* **ANDREW***)* Then please accept my apologies. I took you for one of the Toy-boys she pulls around on her diamonte leashes. *(To* **MARIANNE***)* I'll take these through to the kitchen, shall I? *(Displays her bag of shopping)*

MARIANNE. *(hastily)* No, no. I'll do it. And maybe a nice cup of tea? I'm sure we could all do with one.

ANDREW. *(embarrassed)* Not for me, thanks.

TRYPHOSA. *(bitterly)* I need something stronger than tea after seeing *her* again.

MARIANNE. There's a little sherry in the sideboard.

TRYPHOSA. At this precise moment, I'd prefer cyanide.

CARLA. *(dryly)* Be careful what you wish for, Mother. You might just get it. *(Turns and moving past* **MARIANNE**, *exits in the direction of the kitchen.)*

(There is an embarrassed silence.)

ANDREW. Look. This is obviously not the right moment—

TRYPHOSA. It never *is* when my daughter's around. God knows what I've done to deserve her. I gave her everything. *Everything.* And look at the way she rewards me.

MARIANNE. Tryphosa— *(Moves into the room).*

TRYPHOSA. *(bitterly)* Not an ounce of gratitude. And *you.* I thought you were my friend.

MARIANNE. *(surprised)* I am.

TRYPHOSA. *(hotly)* Then why the pretence? Why not tell me you knew her?

MARIANNE. *(patiently)* Because I don't know her. We'd only met the once before the other day. When you were in hospital, two years ago. And as you'd made it quite clear you weren't on speaking terms, I thought it best to keep quiet. It was none of my business.

TRYPHOSA. *(bitterly)* It obviously didn't stop you keeping in contact with her.

MARIANNE. Only to let her know you were keeping well. Despite what you believe, she does think the world of you.

TRYPHOSA. *(harshly)* Then she's a funny way of showing it. *(Suspiciously)* So why's she here now?

MARIANNE. *(awkwardly)* You'll have to ask her that.

TRYPHOSA. *(glowering)* If she thinks I'm going to reinstate her in my will—

ANDREW. *(glancing at his watch)* I really must be going, Ms Swan. *(To* **MARIANNE***)* Perhaps I could make a proper appointment later? Sometime more convenient?

MARIANNE. *(apologetically)* There's really no need, Mr Perryman. I'm not interested. It's all Tryphosa's idea to trace my family, but I haven't the slightest inclination. *(Smiles)* I know who my parents were, and that's enough for me. I don't see the need for digging around in the past. It's not going to change anything, is it?

ANDREW. Wouldn't your relations be—?

MARIANNE. *(shaking her head gently)* I *have* no relations, Mr Perryman. *(Smiles)* I'm the last of a rather long but unproductive line. *(Apologetically)* Now if you don't mind, I really must get these *(displays her basket)* into the freezer before they melt. *(Turns to exit)*

TRYPHOSA. *(brusquely)* Tell her, Andrew.

MARIANNE. *(pausing and turning back)* Tell me what?

TRYPHOSA. *(flatly)* You may not be as lonely as you think you are.

*(**MARIANNE** stares at her.)*

ANDREW. *(awkwardly)* I did a little preliminary search yesterday. *(Moves upstage towards her)* Your maiden name was Walker, right? And your parents, George and Rebecca? One thirty-seven, Bell Street, Chester?

MARIANNE. *(frowning)* Yes.

ANDREW. There was also a brother? Simon Joseph?

MARIANNE. *(blankly)* Who?

ANDREW. Born in 1927. He'd be seven years old when you were born.

MARIANNE. *(shaking her head)* I'm afraid you're mistaken. I never had a brother. There were just the three of us. Mother, Father and me.

ANDREW. He was christened at St Mary's church, Congleton, in June, 1927.

MARIANNE. *(stunned)* That's impossible. I've never heard of him.

ANDREW. *(frowning)* He could have died, of course. Before you were born.

MARIANNE. *(hotly)* Don't be ridiculous. If I'd had a brother who died, don't you think my parents would have told me about him? Why would they keep it a secret?

ANDREW. *(apologetically)* I only know what the record says. *(Helpfully)* But I can go through the register of deaths. If it was something like scarlet fever...or an accident...

MARIANNE. But it *wasn't*. It couldn't have been. I'd cousins and aunts and my grandmother, yes. But a brother? There wasn't one. I'd have known.

ANDREW. *(gently)* It's there in black and white.

(MARIANNE *looks at him in disbelief, then turns and stumbles blindly out of the room towards the kitchen.)*

(Concerned) Mrs Grayson?

TRYPHOSA. *(dryly)* What did I tell you?

ANDREW. *(turning to her)* I know. And it obviously has given her a shock. But it's not uncommon, Ms Swan. We've traced many histories over the past twelve years, and I can think of several customers who've reacted in the same way. They'd no *idea* there were siblings or other family members and the discovery hit them hard. *(Hastily)* Some were delighted, and couldn't wait to get in contact, but others...well...let's just say the news wasn't exactly welcomed with open arms.

TRYPHOSA. *(frowning)* Why not?

ANDREW. Financial reasons, in the main. Having to share an inheritance with someone they never knew existed. Especially if they've spent most of it. Generally speaking, when families bury their secrets, they hope they'll be hidden forever. *(Hastily)* Not for sinister reasons, of course. If it's a child's death, they simply can't talk about it. It keeps the pain alive. So they blot it out as though it never happened, and get on with their lives.

TRYPHOSA. *(scornfully)* That's ridiculous. *(Sits in the chair right)*

ANDREW. *(forcing a smile)* To you and me, yes. But to those involved... *(He shrugs)*

TRYPHOSA. *(thoughtfully)* So you think he died young? Marianne's brother?

ANDREW. *(shaking his head)* I've no idea. As I said this morning, I'd only time to do a quick search. I won't be at the FRC till later this afternoon, but if she wants me to, I could find out more. It'll all be in there.

TRYPHOSA. *(firmly)* Of course she wants you to. She's *always* regretted being an only child. To find out she had an elder brother…who could still be alive…would be wonderful. And even if he's not…well…at least she'd know what happened to him.

ANDREW. You seem very certain.

TRYPHOSA. I've known her a long time, and know what she wants even before she knows it herself. Trace this brother of hers, and I'll double your fee.

ANDREW. *(frowning)* There's no need for *that*, Ms Swan. My fees—

TRYPHOSA. I'll *insist* upon it, Andrew. Find this Simon Walker, and you'll earn my eternal gratitude.

ANDREW. *(resigned)* I'll do what I can. *(Glances at his watch)* But I really *have* to make a move. *(Moves towards her and picks up his attaché case.)* You'll give my apologies to the ladies?

(TRYPHOSA nods and he moves to the arch)

TRYPHOSA. *(calling)* And don't forget the Kennedy man. Call him as soon as he's home.

(ANDREW nods and exits left. The door is heard to close. A moment later, CARLA enters, carrying a tray which holds four cups and saucers, milk jug and sugar bowl, a cream-filled sponge-cake, side plates, cake forks and tea-spoons. She has removed her suit top to reveal the blouse she had beneath it.)

CARLA. *(frowning)* Was that the door? *(Deposits the tray on the coffee table)*

TRYPHOSA. *(ignoring this)* Where's Marianne?

CARLA. *(glancing around)* Has he gone?

TRYPHOSA. *(tightly)* I asked you a question.

CARLA. *(unconcerned)* *I* asked you *two*.

TRYPHOSA. *(fumes and rises)* This is ridiculous.

CARLA. *(moving down left)* It usually *is* when trying to have a conversation with you. If you're not in the middle of the spotlight, you stuff your ears with cotton wool and switch off. *(Bitterly)* I don't even know why I'm bothering. If I'd any sense, I'd have stayed in New York and only come back for the funeral.

TRYPHOSA. *(frowning)* What funeral? What are you talking about?

CARLA. *(turning to her)* Much as it pains to admit it, Mother, I don't want to see you dead.

TRYPHOSA. *(baffled)* Dead?

CARLA. *(glowering)* If anyone's going to kill you, I want it to be me. After all these years, I think I've earned that right.

TRYPHOSA. *(tartly)* Don't be so melodramatic. *(Moves down right)* Who'd want to kill *me?*

CARLA. *(sarcastically)* Do you have a spare hour so I can list them? *(Scornfully)* But don't worry. When your time *does* come, I'll make sure it's entirely from *natural* causes. *(Sits in the easy chair, left)*

TRYPHOSA. *(scathingly)* You're out of your mind. *(Angrily)* What are you *doing* here? Go back to America and leave me in peace.

CARLA. *(firmly)* Not till I know you're safe. Like it or lump it, I'm staying here till I'm satisfied.

TRYPHOSA. *(shocked)* She's letting you stay here? In Cooper's View?

CARLA. *(impatiently)* Of course not. I wouldn't *dream* of imposing myself.

TRYPHOSA. *(scornfully)* That'll be a first. You've been imposing yourself into *my* life since the day you were born. Why should Marianne be spared?

*(Enter **MARIANNE**, looking unsteady. She carries a teapot.)*

MARIANNE. Spared what? *(Looks round)* Where's Mr Perryman?

TRYPHOSA. He had to leave. But it's all been taken care of. If you *did* have a brother, he'll find out what happened to him and why it's been kept a secret all these years.

MARIANNE. But I *didn't,* Tryphosa. I know I didn't. *(Puts the teapot down on the coffee table and sits on the sofa)* There must be a mix-up of some kind.

TRYPHOSA. *(reassuringly)* Well he'll soon sort it out. I've every confidence in him. *(Frowns)* But what if there *is*...or *was* a brother? What are you going to do?

MARIANNE. *(protesting)* I won't be doing anything. How many times do I have to say it? *(With great emphasis)* I have no brother. I never did have. *(Brushes her forehead absently)*

TRYPHOSA. *(staring at her)* Are you feeling all right? You're grey as a goose.

MARIANNE. Just shaken, that's all. *(Begins sorting out the cups)* And I can't find my pills. Lord knows what I've done with them. *(Frowns)* I could have sworn they were on my bedside cabinet. It's where I usually keep them. *(Pours tea)*

CARLA. Are they important?

MARIANNE. *(shaking her head)* Just something to take when I'm feeling a bit wobbly. Blood pressure, so they tell me. Though at my age they can always find something they're unhappy about. If it weren't for people like me, half the chemists in the country would be closed. *(Lifts a cup to hand it to her)* Milk and sugar?

CARLA. *(shaking her head)* Straight from the pot.

(Rises to take the cup, returning to the chair after she's done so. **MARIANNE** *adds milk and sugar to one of the other cups.)*

TRYPHOSA. So when did you take them last? These pills of yours?

MARIANNE. *(dismissively)* I don't know. A few days ago, I think. I'm not exactly popping them on a regular basis. *(Hands the cup to* **TRYPHOSA**)

CARLA. But shouldn't you be? I mean, Harvey...my husband...has blood pressure problems, and takes them daily.

TRYPHOSA. *(moving right)* I'm not surprised. Being married to you.

MARIANNE. *(ignoring this)* I should, of course. You're quite right. *(Adds milk to her cup)* But I hate taking medication. Always have done. If I can manage without it, I do. *(Amused)* Not like my late husband. I don't think there was anything he wouldn't take to stay healthy. *(Wryly)* Not that it did him much good. He was only sixty-seven when he died.

TRYPHOSA. *(sitting in the chair, right)* So much for creaking gates. *(Sips at her tea and frowns)* What kind of tea's this?

MARIANNE. Just the normal kind. Why?

TRYPHOSA. It tastes odd.

MARIANNE. *(cautiously sips at her own and grimaces)* You're right. It *does* taste strange.

CARLA. *(sipping her own tea)* It's alright to me.

MARIANNE. *(puzzled)* It must be the milk, then. But I only opened it this morning. *(Peers into the cup)*

TRYPHOSA. *(shuddering)* Oh. I can't drink this, Marianne. *(Holds the cup out to* **MARIANNE***)*

MARIANNE. *(putting her own cup on the tray)* Of course not. *(Rises and takes* **TRYPHOSA***'s cup)* I'll make us some fresh. I've another carton in the fridge. *(Puts the cup on the tray)*

TRYPHOSA. It's made me feel quite sick.

MARIANNE. *(picking up the tray)* I'm so sorry. Would you like a little brandy?

TRYPHOSA. *(distressed)* I could do with something.

MARIANNE. *(embarrassed)* I'll just take these through to the kitchen and— *(Her face contorts and she quickly replaces the tray on the coffee table.)* Oh. *(Sways slightly)* Oh dear. *(Subsides heavily onto the sofa)*

CARLA. *(concerned)* What is it? What's wrong?

MARIANNE. *(faintly)* I don't know. I feel…*odd.* *(Slumps sideways and lies still.)*

*(*TRYPHOSA *and* CARLA *rise in alarm.)*

TRYPHOSA. *(concerned)* Marianne?

CARLA. Mrs Grayson?

TRYPHOSA. *(to* **CARLA***)* Call an ambulance. Quickly.

CARLA. *(uncertain)* What?

TRYPHOSA. *(impatiently)* Never mind. I'll do it myself. *(Snatches up her bag and roots inside it)* Where *is* the bloody thing? *(Tosses out the contents, willy-nilly)*

CARLA. What are you looking for?

TRYPHOSA. *(snapping)* What do you *think* I'm looking for? My mobile, of course... *(Stops in mid speech looking startled)* Ohhhhh. *(She sways unsteadily and the bag slips out of her hand.)*

CARLA. Mother?

TRYPHOSA. *(in disbelief)* We've been *poisoned*. *(Totters backwards to the easy chair)*

CARLA. *(scornfully)* Don't be ridiculous.

*(***TRYPHOSA** *sinks heavily into the easy chair)*

TRYPHOSA. *(fighting to stay conscious)* It's *you*. You've done this, you bitch. *(Gasps in pain)* But don't think you'll get away with it. *(Savagely)* I'll see you in hell first. *(Gives another gasp and slumps in the chair, unconscious.)*

CARLA. *(uncertainly)* Mother? *(Quickly puts her cup on the coffee table and moves to* **TRYPHOSA***'s side.)* Mother? *(Shakes her)*

(There is no response.)

(Softly) Oh, my God.

(Backs away, hesitates, then turns and exits quickly through the arch towards the kitchen. The lights fade rapidly to end the scene and Act One.)

ACT TWO

Scene One

(Afternoon. Eight days later.)

(The room is virtually unchanged, but the flower vase has gone and the tea things have been cleared. The french windows are open, and **FRANK** *sits in the chair right, reading a newspaper. After a moment,* **AMY** *enters through the arch carrying the vase which is now full of fresh flowers. Her face is still pale, but the black eye has vanished, and she now wears a two-piece suit and blouse. She crosses to the cabinet, places the vase in its usual position, then stands back to consider it.)*

AMY. *(to* **FRANK***)* What do you think?

FRANK. *(still reading, and disinterested)* Mm?

AMY. To the flowers.

FRANK. *(still immersed)* What about them?

AMY. Do you think she'll like them?

FRANK. *(irritably)* How should *I* know?

AMY. *(stung)* You could at least *look* at them.

FRANK. *(lowering the paper, testily)* Are you blind or something? I'm reading the paper.

AMY. *(annoyed)* Well I'm not doing this for my own benefit, you know. A bit of help wouldn't go amiss. She'll be here soon.

FRANK. *(sarcastically)* Well whoop-de-doo-doo. Get me the hammer and nails and I'll lay the red carpet. Or would you prefer me to polish the silver?

AMY. *(hurt)* There's no need for sarcasm. I'm only trying to make things look nice. She can't have been happy in that place.

FRANK. *(returning to the newspaper)* I didn't hear her complaining.

AMY. *(tartly)* That's because you've only seen her once since the day she went in. It's me who's done the visiting. I've hardly been out of the place this past week. *(Distressed)* I can't understand it. What kind of maniac would poison the milk in a supermarket? *Anyone* could drink it.

FRANK. *(lowering the paper again)* Quite a few *did*, according to this. *(Rattles the newspaper)* Family in Wilson Street, pensioner in Park Road, young couple in Arneside Crescent, and eighteen more at a coffee morning in the Town Hall. *(Grins)* Pity the Mayor missed all the fun. I'd have given a week's wages to see that prat having his gold-plated stomach pumped.

AMY. *(sharply)* It's not funny, Frank.

FRANK. *(glowering)* I didn't say it was. But I don't see why you're getting your knickers in a twist about it. They haven't died, have they? It just had 'em tossing their cookies. A few days in bed and they were right as rain.

AMY. *(tightly)* Except for my mother, who's still in a coma.

FRANK. Well don't expect me to shed crocodile tears. If she doesn't come round, we're home and dry. I've searched the house, top to bottom, and if she *has* made a new will, she's got it well hidden.

AMY. *(maliciously)* She could have asked someone else to look after it for her.

FRANK. *(smirking)* Do you think I hadn't thought of that? The only one she'd trust is old mother Grayson...so while you've been doing your Florence Nightingale act, I've been through this place with a tooth-comb. And nada. Not a thing.

(The door chime sounds.)

AMY. *(startled)* It's them. They're here already.

FRANK. *(glancing at his watch)* Can't be. It's only twenty past.

AMY. Who else could it be? *(Hurries out and vanishes left)*

(FRANK scowls and quickly folds the paper, stuffing it down the side of the chair before standing and facing the arch)

ANDREW. *(off)* Mrs Beverage? *(Warmly)* Andrew Perryman. Heritage Research. We spoke on the phone.

AMY. *(off)* Oh... Yes... Of course.

ANDREW. *(off)* Has there been any change? *(Pause)* I'm *so* sorry.

(He appears in the arch.)

It must have been a terrible shock. I couldn't believe it myself when I heard.

(AMY appears beside him.)

But as long as she's holding on... *(Notices FRANK)* Oh.

AMY. *(hastily introducing them.)* My husband. Frank. *(To FRANK)* Mr Perryman. From the research firm I told you about.

(FRANK scowls.)

ANDREW. *(entering the room and moving center behind the sofa)* How do you do? *(Extends his hand to FRANK)* I can't tell you how sorry I am. It must be a nightmare for you.

AMY. *(moving into the room)* How did you know we were here?

ANDREW. *(turning to her)* I called at the house, and your gardener told me. Mrs Grayson's coming home today. Yes?

FRANK. *(ignoring the outstretched hand)* And what's it to do with *you?*

AMY. *(embarrassed)* Frank.

ANDREW. *(turning back to FRANK)* I'm doing some research for Ms Swan. And I've come across something odd. *(Realises FRANK is not going to shake his hand and drops it)*

FRANK. *(frowning)* Odd? What kind of odd?

ANDREW. *(awkwardly)* I'm afraid that's between your mother-in-law and myself, Mr Beverage. She *is* the client, you understand?

FRANK. Yes. *(Pointedly)* But you'll not get much out of her for the next few weeks. Even if she does come round. *(Sits again)* Could be brain damaged, for all we know. Funny things, comas. You never can tell what damage's been done till folk snap out of 'em.

ANDREW. Which is why I'm hoping Mrs Grayson can shed some light.

FRANK. *(suspiciously)* And what would *she* know, that we don't?

AMY. *(blurting)* If it's about the Kennedys...?

ANDREW. *(turning to her)* I'm sorry?

AMY. She *told* me. In the hospital.

(**ANDREW** *looks blank.*)

You're trying to trace my mother's real mother.

ANDREW. *(awkwardly)* That *is* one of the things I'm researching. Yes. But—

FRANK. *(scornfully)* Can't see the point of it, myself. You are who you are, in my opinion. And what difference will it make to her *now*? She's seventy-four years old and might *never* come round. If you ask me, it's a waste of time and money.

ANDREW. *(mildly)* We should *all* know our family histories, Mr Beverage.

FRANK. Well you'd say that, wouldn't you? It's how you make your money. Chasing up the dead and buried. But if my Great gran was Madam Butterfly, it wouldn't make me a Chinaman, would it? As I said... You are what you are, and the rest of it doesn't matter.

AMY. *(quickly)* Can I offer you some tea, Mr Perryman?

ANDREW. No, thank you. *(Lightly)* I've been forgoing milk since the news came out. *(Apologetically)* It must seem ridiculous, but until they catch this madman—

AMY. *(agreeing)* I know what you mean. It was only a few bottles, according to the police…and all from the same supermarket…but sales have dropped all over town. I don't know how people are managing. We still have ours delivered, so we know that's safe, thank goodness. I brought a bottle over.

FRANK. *(interrupting)* So have you found her, then? Tryphosa's mother?

ANDREW. Not yet, I'm afraid. But I'm meeting Mr Kennedy this weekend. They're finally back from holiday.

AMY. *(indicating the sofa)* Won't you sit down?

ANDREW. Thank you. *(Moves round and sits on the sofa)* I'm sure he'll be helpful. Though your mother's insistence he may be related seems most unlikely, if you don't mind my saying so.

FRANK. *(bluntly)* And what if he isn't helpful?

ANDREW. *(shrugging)* Then I just keep on digging.

FRANK. *(pointedly)* So even if she doesn't come round, you're not giving up?

ANDREW. *(frowning)* I'm hoping it won't come to that, Mr Beverage.

FRANK. *(pressing)* But if it does? If she *does* kick the bucket. What happens then?

ANDREW. *(uncomfortably)* Our agreement ends, of course. Unless the family *wish* us to continue the search. We'd submit our bill to the executors for work carried out… minus the advance payment she made…and that would be that. But I'm sure there'll be no question of—

FRANK. *(cutting in)* Then you've more faith in hospitals than I have. Eight days she's been unconscious. It's only the machines that are keeping her alive.

AMY. *(frowning)* We can't understand it. None of the others were affected like this. Once they'd had treatment, they were fine.

ANDREW. *(nodding)* It depends how much she absorbed, I expect. *And* if it clashed with anything else she might have been taking. Some drugs can be *deadly* if they're mixed with others. *(In wonder)* I can't believe the stupidity. No matter *what* their grudge is against the supermarkets, to inject barbituates into the milk is past belief. What if they'd used cyanide...or arsenic?

FRANK. *(scowling)* Then we wouldn't be wondering if we'd still have a roof over our heads the minute her will's read.

ANDREW. *(puzzled)* I'm sorry?

FRANK. *(leaning forward)* It's not public knowledge, but since she had her stroke a few years back, she's been having problems. *(Taps his temple with his index finger)* Half her time, she doesn't know if she's on this earth or Fuller's.

*(**AMY** looks dismayed.)*

ANDREW. *(frowning)* Really? That wasn't the impression I got. Quite the opposite, in fact.

FRANK. That's because you don't know her like *we* do. *(Settling back)* She's always been a fighter, Tryphosa has. Wouldn't have got where she was, if she hadn't been able to give as good as she got. *(Regretfully)* But when the mind starts playing tricks...that's when paranoia sets in. Didn't trust anyone after it happened. Not even us...her own family. *(To **AMY**)* Isn't that right, Amy? *(To **ANDREW**)* Thought we were all out to "get" her.

AMY. *(embarrassed)* It wasn't that bad, Frank.

FRANK. *(easily)* So why was she always making new wills? One week everything was going to Oxfam, and the next it was Battersea Dogs' Home, the Chelsea Pensioners, or Save the bloody Whales. She left Covent Garden fifty million 'til they announced Massenet's *Manon*, instead of Puccini's *Manon Lescaut*. She was writing out a new will before the paste on the posters had a chance to dry. *(Heavily)* No. There were no second chances with

Tryphosa. Once you were out of favour, you were out for good.

ANDREW. *(frowning)* But surely she'd no argument with *you?*

FRANK. You wouldn't have thought so. After all we've done for her. But she's got this weird idea I've been beating up Amy, so who knows? Until her latest will's read, we're all in limbo. *(To* AMY*)* Aren't we love? *(To* ANDREW*)* This time next week, we could be out on the streets.

AMY. *(hastily)* Are you sure you wouldn't like tea? It won't take a minute.

FRANK. *(to* ANDREW; *easily)* What is it with women and tea? *(To* AMY*)* He's already *said.* *(To* ANDREW*)* We've only been here two hours and my back teeth are floating. She's in and out of that kitchen like a fiddler's elbow. *(To* AMY*)* For God's sake sit down...or go and bake a cake or something.

AMY. *(glancing suddenly at the arch)* That's them. They're here. *(Hurries out and heads left)*

*(*FRANK *rises from the chair.)*

(Off: warmly) Mrs Grayson.

CARLA. *(off)* Give me a hand with the wheelchair.

AMY. *(off: gushingly)* How are you feeling? Do you need a hand to get up?

CARLA. *(off)* Don't *pull* at her, Amy. Take the blanket.

*(*AMY *backs into view clutching a travel blanket.)*

AMY. I'll put the kettle on, shall I? You'll be wanting a drink.

CARLA. *(off)* Have you made up the bed?

AMY. *(nodding)* As soon as we got here. It's all ready.

MARIANNE. *(Off: Lightly)* Oh, for goodness' sake. I'm not on my last legs yet. *(Appears in the archway)*

(She is dressed in a light summer dress and appears slightly unsteady on her feet.)

And there was no need for the wheelchair. I'm quite capable of... *(Notices* **FRANK** *and* **ANDREW**) Mr Perryman. Frank.

FRANK. *(crossing to her)* Mrs Grayson. Welcome home. Let me help you. *(He assists her to the armchair left.)* You've no idea how worried we've been.

MARIANNE. *(dismissively)* Oh, go on, with you. It's Tryphosa you should be worried about. *(Concerned)* Has she come out of her coma, yet? *(Sits heavily)*

AMY. *(hurrying forward downstage left and draping the blanket over* **MARIANNE***'s lap)* Not that we've heard. And the doctors don't seem to care. Nobody does. Except us.

MARIANNE. *(frowning)* Shouldn't you be there? At the hospital?

FRANK. They said there was no point. They'd call us if anything changed.

MARIANNE. *(looking at* **ANDREW***, askance)* And Mr Perryman?

ANDREW. *(smiling)* I'd heard you were being discharged, and hoped you'd be able to help me. With your family tree.

MARIANNE. *(protesting faintly)* But I've already said.

FRANK. *(cutting in)* Well it's nothing to do with me, but I don't see that now's the time to go into that. She needs to get over this poisoning first. Plenty of rest and relaxation. Build up her resources. *(Stands behind the armchair)*

ANDREW. It'll only take a moment.

*(**CARLA** enters. She wears an expensive looking suit)*

CARLA. *(harshly)* Which part of "not now" is difficult, Mr Perryman? I thought we'd agreed there'd be no need for further work until Mother's out of danger? *(She crosses right to the music centre.)* We'll contact you, if and when that's established.

ANDREW. *(mildly)* With all due respect, Mrs— *(Falters, then recovers)* This particular search has nothing to do with your mother. And it's something that greatly concerns

Mrs Grayson. *(To* **MARIANNE***)* I know you believe you were an only child, but there's no question about it. You *did* have an elder brother, and the reason you knew nothing about it is because he was put up for fostering a few days after his birth.

(**MARIANNE** *stares at him in disbelief.*)

(Quietly) A couple from Congleton took him…a Mrs and Mrs Neil…They were quite well known in the area. Very highly thought of.

MARIANNE. *(dazedly)* No.

ANDREW. I did quite a lot of research during your hospital stay… Ms Swan had been most insistent…and was lucky enough to find a few people who remembered. Your old English teacher in Chester, for instance… Miss Jenkins.

MARIANNE. *(surprised)* What?

ANDREW. She's in a nursing home now. Near Grosvenor Park. Over a hundred, but still sharp as a tack. And sends her regards, by the way. Then there was a chap who'd been at school with Simon, in Congleton. Remembered him well. Top of the class in everything, he said, and if it hadn't been for his shyness and the unfortunate facial problem, he'd have been head boy without question.

AMY. Facial problem?

ANDREW. The reason he was fostered, I'm assuming. *(Uneasily to* **MARIANNE***)* He'd a rather noticeable naevus that covered most of his face. From what I understand, it was only his right eye that wasn't affected. The rest was sort of dark purple and lumpy.

(**MARIANNE** *looks stunned.*)

(Grimaces) Must have gone through hell, poor kid. They couldn't do much about it in those days. *(Hastily)* But he wasn't bullied. Not according to my source. He was too well liked.

FRANK. *(sourly)* Good job he didn't go to my school. You could get your head punched in for having the wrong hairstyle.

CARLA. *(noticing* MARIANNE*: anxiously)* Marianne?

AMY. Mrs Grayson? *(Gently touches her on the left shoulder)*

(MARIANNE *snaps out of it and looks at* ANDREW.*)*

MARIANNE. *(anxiously)* And what happened to him? Where did he go?

ANDREW. *(apologetically)* Died in 1996.

MARIANNE. *(after a short silence, softly)* I never knew. They didn't tell me. *(More strongly)* All these years and I'd no idea. No idea at all.

ANDREW. I realise it's come as a shock, but—

MARIANNE. No. No. *(More herself)* I mean yes. It has been a shock. But it all fits in, doesn't it? *(Forcing a smile)* She was always obsessive…my mother. Couldn't bear to have anything out of place. Everything had to be perfect. *(Remembering)* The pleats in the curtains…the right flowers in the right vases…everything immaculate from morning to night. *(Softly)* No wonder she gave him away. It must have torn her apart, every time she looked at him.

ANDREW. *(hesitantly)* There *is* something else.

(MARIANNE *looks at him.)*

A family. He married a girl from Mossley and had three children. Two girls and a boy.

MARIANNE. *(eyes widening)* Children?

ANDREW. They'd be easy to trace if you wanted to…

MARIANNE. *(animated)* Oh, yes. Yes. You've got to find them for me. I want to meet them.
(Dazedly) Two nieces and a nephew. *(To* ANDREW *again)* You must find them. You must.

ANDREW. I'll do my best.

CARLA. *(firmly)* I think that's enough for now, Mr Perryman. *(Crosses to* MARIANNE*)* She's just out of hospital in case you'd forgotten, and I need to get her upstairs. *(Attempts to help* **MARIANNE** *stand)*

MARIANNE. *(refusing to do so)* No, no. I'm all right. I want to know more.

CARLA. And you will, later. You're white as a sheet and as cold as ice. The sooner we get you to bed, the better.

MARIANNE. *(fiercely)* I don't want to go to bed. Leave me alone. I want to know more about my family.

*(***CARLA*** *glares fiercely at* **ANDREW.***)*

ANDREW. *(hastily)* I'll call again tomorrow. With anything else I find out. *(Glances at his watch)* I'm in rather a hurry at the moment, and I've told you all I know so far. *(Pointedly)* I could have a lot more by tomorrow. *(Rises)*

MARIANNE. *(hopefully)* Do you promise?

ANDREW. *(earnestly)* Scout's honour. *(Gives a Scout salute)*

CARLA. *(to* **MARIANNE***)* Then that's settled. A good night's rest to get you used to being home again, and he'll be back in the morning. I'm sure Amy can see him out while I help you up the stairs. *(Assists her to stand, handing the blanket to* **AMY.***)* Easy does it.
(Escorts **MARIANNE** *out of the room)* We'll have a hot drink for you as soon as you're comfortable.

(They vanish from sight.)

FRANK. *(to* **ANDREW***, dryly)* I take it there's no mistake. It's all above board, this mysterious family thing? I mean…I'd hate to think it was some kind of scam to get money from a vulnerable old woman. I wouldn't like that all all. *(To* **AMY***)* Would I, Amy?

ANDREW. *(coldly)* There's nothing of a scam about it, Mr Beverage. The information I and my company gather can all be confirmed at the FRC, or from documentation and taped interviews. For the past ten years…

FRANK. *(giving a shark-like smile)* Well that's all right, then, isn't it? I was just making sure. After all, I do have a vested interest, so to speak. *(Pointedly)* What with my mother-in-law footing the bill, and all that.

ANDREW. *(after a short pause)* I'd...better be off. As I said earlier, I *am* in a hurry. *(Moves towards the arch then hesitates)* But I'd appreciate it if you'd let me know of any change in Ms Swan's condition.

FRANK. *(easily)* And how'd we do that? You seem to pop in and out like a jack-in-the box.

ANDREW. I'll give you a card. *(Does so)*

FRANK. *(glancing at it)* Work from home, do you?

ANDREW. No need for expensive offices in my line of work. I can cope quite well in my spare room. *(Indicates the card)* Phone numbers, fax, e-mail and address. And if you want to leave a message, there's always the machine.

FRANK. *(smirking)* We'll be in touch, then.

ANDREW. *(nodding to AMY)* Mrs Beverage. *(Exits through the arch)*

FRANK. *(savagely)* Tosser. *(Moves down right, dropping the card on the table behind the sofa)* I should have ripped his bloody face off.

AMY. *(puzzled)* Frank?

FRANK. Don't you see it? Thanks to him, we're going to be back exactly where we started from.

AMY. *(puzzled)* I don't understand.

FRANK. *(snarling)* Of course you don't. But I do. *(Glowering)* Now he's come up with a bunch of lost family, we can say goodbye to the old girl's money. She's not going to leave us anything with them rattling their poor boxes under her nose. We've been shafted.

AMY. *(protesting)* We don't know that, Frank.

FRANK. *(harshly)* Don't we? And what do we do if she suddenly decides your mother's money would be far better off in their pockets than in ours?

AMY. She wouldn't.

FRANK. *(sneering)* And you know that for a fact, do you? Well pardon my cynicism, but I'm not taking the chance. If anyone's getting their hands on your mother's money, it's me. I'll make damn sure of that. Damn sure. *(Heads for the arch)*

AMY. *(uncertainly)* What are you going to do?

FRANK. *(halting and turning)* What do you think? *(Gives a nasty smile)* I'm going to see a man. About a dog. *(He exits)*

(AMY stands in silence, looking at the arch. After a moment, CARLA enters.)

CARLA. *(coolly)* Something wrong?

AMY. *(uncertainly)* No. *(More firmly)* No.

CARLA. *(moving behind the sofa)* You never did make a good liar, Amy. *(Quoting)* Beware thy sins should seek thee out. *(Seats herself on the sofa, right)*

AMY. *(defensively)* And what's *that* supposed to mean? *(Moves down right of armchair)*

CARLA. *(dryly)* Does it need spelling out? *(Glowering)* He's up to something, isn't he?

(AMY prepares to speak.)

Don't bother denying it. I know him too well. *(Giving a wry smile)* Not that it matters. He'll pay for it this time. *(With grim satisfaction)* Oh, yes. And won't I enjoy it?

AMY. *(quietly)* And what about me? *(Sitting left of her on the sofa)* What am *I* going to do?

CARLA. *(firmly)* Get on with your life.

AMY. *(protesting)* But—

CARLA. *(harshly)* No buts about it. With *him* out of the way, you can live a normal life. Or at least one that's as normal as someone in our family can manage. *(Bitterly)* I should have killed him thirty years ago. Not wait till now to do something.

AMY. *(defensively)* It hasn't *all* been bad. We had some good times.

CARLA. *(scornfully)* Oh, yes. You must have *loved* those broken ribs in Sardinia…and the wrist in New Zealand. Not to mention the lost teeth and broken nose in Toronto. How you kept them from Mother, I'll never know.

AMY. *(quietly)* She wasn't always there.

CARLA. *(tiredly)* No. She never *was* there, was she? Not when we wanted her most. *(Bitterly)* Too busy chasing the applause. *(Distantly)* And now look at her.

AMY. *(after a moment)* Is she going to recover, you think?

CARLA. *(sighing)* God knows. They're doing all they can, but it's over a week now. If she *was* going to come round, I'd have thought she'd have done it by this time.

AMY. It could be months, according to the doctor.

CARLA. *(with determination)* All the more reason for doing what we have to do, *now*. I'll arrange for someone to look after Mrs Grayson while we're out, and first thing in the morning…

(She stops speaking and gets out her mobile phone.)

Hello? *(Pause)* Speaking. *(Pause)* We'll be there right away. *(Looks stunned and ends the call)*. It's the hospital. She died a few minutes ago.

AMY. *(stunned)* No.

CARLA. *(rising)* I'll call a cab. There's a list in the kitchen. *(Hurries towards the arch)*

AMY. *(brokenly, as she rises)* I'll tell Mrs Grayson.

CARLA. *(as she exits)* I should have been there. I should have *been* there.

(AMY moves right, round the sofa and behind it. About to follow CARLA, she notices the card that FRANK put down, stops and picks it up. For a moment she looks at it blankly, then replaces it and exits, a curious expression on her face. There is a short pause, then the curtain closes for the end of the scene.)

Scene Two

(Late the next morning.)

(The room is unchanged, but the windows are closed and the sky is overcast. **MARIANNE,** *in a dark dress and slippers, sits on the sofa, a shawl around her shoulders and a far away expression on her face. An opened music magazine is on her lap. An untouched cup of tea is on the coffee table in front of her. After a moment,* **FRANK** *appears in the arch, minus his jacket, and stands for a moment, observing her.)*

FRANK. *(finally)* Everything all right, Mrs G? Not feeling ill again?

MARIANNE. *(looking at him, blankly)* No, no. Just... remembering.

FRANK. *(moving behind the sofa, heading right)* Yes. *(With mock heaviness)* We're going to miss the old girl, aren't we? They don't make 'em like her any more. Broke the mould after that one. Best *Tosca* I ever saw. *(Forcing a grin)* Though her *Butterfly* was more like a bee. *(Sits in the chair right)*

MARIANNE. *(smiling sadly)* It wasn't her finest role, was it? She much preferred the ones with a bit of fire in them. But the public loved it. And I don't think she let *Puccini* down.

FRANK. Probably bending his ear, right now. Telling him how much she improved it.

*(***MARIANNE*** begins sobbing quietly.)*

(Lightly) Hey. Hey. No need for tears. She wouldn't want *that*, you know.

MARIANNE. *(attempting to recover)* I know. *(Wipes at her eyes)* It's just...the thought of not *seeing* her again. We'd been friends for so long. And now she's gone.

FRANK. *(lightly)* But not forgotten, eh? She'll never be forgotten.

MARIANNE. *(pulling herself together)* I don't know why I'm getting in such a state. I can't imagine what the girls are going through. *(Adjusts her shawl)*

FRANK. *(agreeing)* Press were at the hospital before they arrived. How they got hold of it, I'll never know. Probably one of the nurses called 'em. *(Scornfully)* Bloody vultures. One got in the back way and was in her room clicking away with his *mobile* before the staff had time to throw him out. Be on the front page this morning. Take it from me.

MARIANNE. *(nodding)* It was on the television, a while ago.

FRANK. They were outside the house all night, too. *(Scornfully)* Kept knocking on the door and asking to use the toilet. *(Smirks)* I gave 'em "use the toilet" all right. Turned on all the garden sprinklers and doused the bloody lot of 'em. We sneaked out the back way while they were trying to dry themselves off, and booked in at the Best Western with Carla. Probably stay there till after the funeral, now. *(Thoughtfully)* Must be shaking in his shoes, eh?

MARIANNE. *(puzzled)* Who must?

FRANK. The nutter who poisoned the milk. I mean, it's not just a nasty trick, now, is it? It's murder. And, much as it hurts me to say it, *you* could have been in the same boat if it hadn't been for Carla. Thank God she was here and called for help.

MARIANNE. *(nodding)* I owe her my life.

FRANK. *(hastily)* But don't let her catch you saying that. Got an eye for the main chance, that one. She might come at you for some kind of reward.

*(**MARIANNE** looks puzzled.)*

Don't get me wrong, Mrs G., but I've known her for thirty years or so, and like they say...leopards don't change their spots. She can sniff out a bank account quicker than she could a gas leak. And let's face it. With her mother's millions in your back pocket, you could buy and sell little Carla…and that precious husband of hers.

MARIANNE. *(frowning)* But I won't *have* Tryphosa's money. The girls are sharing it.

FRANK. Well I know you said that a while back, but she's not the trusting type, our Carla. Now you've turned up a long lost brother, she might start thinking you wouldn't want *his* family to lose out. Blood being thicker than water, and all that.

MARIANNE. I won't change my mind, if *that's* what you're thinking. *(Firmly)* I don't want a penny of Tryphosa's money, and now she's gone, there's no further need for our little deception. If she didn't change her will, I'll simply re-make my own again and have more than enough to leave to Simon's family, should I wish to do so. *(Frowning)* But how you can even *think* about money with Tryphosa hardly cold, I can't…

FRANK. *(cutting in)* Just wanting you to to be on your guard, Mrs G. It's my *job*, you see? Financial security. Remember? *(Rises)* You're a very nice woman, but in my opinion, your heart rules your head. Exactly the right type to be taken advantage of. And even if I'm wrong about Carla, you could have problems in other directions. Once the news gets out, the world and its wife'll be sending you begging letters. *(Moves towards her)* You wouldn't believe the ones Tryphosa got. Never a day went by.

MARIANNE. *(uncertainly)* But there won't *be* any news. Why should there be?

FRANK. *(lightly)* There's bound to be publicity. Fifty-odd million's not chicken-feed. Every pig in the country'll be trying to get its snout in the trough.

MARIANNE. *(protesting weakly)* But as I'm refusing it in favour of Carla and Amy, there's no need for anyone to know I even existed.

FRANK. *(amused)* I'm afraid it don't work that way, Mrs G. Freedom of information, see? Once the will's read, it'll be public property. And you know what the public's like? If they hear Tryphosa left you her fortune, who'll believe you didn't want it and gave it back to her family? *(Moves upstage and moves left)* One way or another, the press'll be buzzing round here like flies, ringing the doorbell and shouting through the letterbox twenty-four seven. If you'll take *my* advice, you'll go into hiding for the next few weeks until the fuss dies down. Take a nice long holiday.

MARIANNE. *(distressed)* But I can't leave Cooper's View. What about my garden? Who'd look after that?

FRANK. *(easily)* You could get someone in. *(Hesitates)* Though it might be a waste of time. They're not exactly careful where they're planting their feet, the dear old press wallahs. You should see the borders at *our* place. Gardener's tearing his hair out.

MARIANNE. *(hopefully)* Perhaps if I talked it over with the girls…?

(CARLA appears in the arch. She is wearing dark clothes for mourning and looks dreadful.)

CARLA. Talked *what* over?

(MARIANNE looks flustered)

FRANK. *(cutting in)* A break. For Mrs Grayson. A few weeks abroad, or something.

(CARLA looks at him icily for a moment, then begins to unfasten her coat.)

CARLA. *(to MARIANNE)* Have you anywhere in mind? Or do you just want to get away? There's the villa in Calabria, if you're interested. *(To FRANK)* Assuming she still had it?

(FRANK nods.)

MARIANNE. Calabria?

CARLA. Southern Italy. I used to live there. Back in the seventies. *(Throws a look of scorn at FRANK)* With Guido. *(Takes her coat off and drapes it on the back of the chair left)*

He rented it from a local landowner till Mother found out where I was, bought the place up behind our backs and served us notice to leave.

*(**MARIANNE** looks dismayed.)*

(Amused) What she didn't know was that we'd already decided to go our separate ways. By the time the letter arrived, Guido was about to head for Rome again and *I* was in the States. We laughed like drains when we realized. *(Moves down left)* But it all turned out for the best. Like us, she simply loved the place, and whenever she sang in Italy, it's where she'd stay. The views are out of this world. *(Sits heavily in the armchair)*

MARIANNE. *(concerned)* It's very kind of you, dear, but it's *you* who should be thinking of a break. Not me. You've been through an awful few days, and I don't know how you've coped. I was almost dis-functional when Gerald was dying. And afterwards...

(She shakes her head slowly.)

CARLA. *(ignoring this)* Will you say a few words at her funeral? I think she'd like that.

MARIANNE. *(startled)* Oh. *(Bites her lip)* I don't know that I *could*. What if I break down? I mean...I wouldn't want... Not in front of everyone.

CARLA. *(reassuringly)* It'll only be family. And perhaps a few reps from the opera companies.

FRANK. *(moving right)* Rest of 'em won't be let near the place. Fans and gutter press. Get them inside the church and the whole thing'd become a free-for-all.

MARIANNE. *(to **CARLA**)* Wouldn't it be better if you—? Or Amy—?

FRANK. *(amused)* No use asking Amy. She'd never get the words out. She'll be blubbering all over the place. And as for Carla... *(Smiles nastily at **CARLA**)* Well...we all knew how *they* got on with each other. It'd seem a bit hypocritical if *she* started spouting Tryphosa's merits.

CARLA. *(ignoring this)* You don't have to do it. It's only if you feel. I'm not twisting your arm, or anything.

MARIANNE. *(reluctantly)* I suppose I could manage a few words... *(Remembering)* There was a poem someone read at my husband's funeral. Not at all maudlin, you understand . Just very, very comforting. I asked for a copy, afterwards. It's in my drawer, upstairs, I think. I showed it to your mother once and she said she liked it, too. I'll look it out, shall I?

FRANK. *(easily)* Good idea. Might appeal to Amy, as well. Likes a bit of poetry, she does. Providing it's none of this modern rubbish. No June rhyming with October. *(To CARLA)* Where is she, by the way? Not left her in town, have you?

CARLA. *(acidly)* I imagine she's at the florists. There's still things to be done, you know. We've been on our feet since eight this morning.

MARIANNE. *(flustered)* I'll make us some tea. *(Rises)*

FRANK. *(quickly)* Don't bother for me, Mrs G. I'll pop down there and see if I can find her. She shouldn't be on her own at a time like this. *(Looking at CARLA)* Some people can take it in their stride... especially when there's no real feeling involved...but ones like Amy need all the support they can get. *(Sweetly)* Wouldn't you say so, Carla?

CARLA. *(glaring)* With *you* around, she could end up needing life support.

FRANK. *(glowers at her, then smiles)* You never give up, do you? *(Lightly)* Well think what you like, but Mrs G here knows the truth. I wouldn't hurt Amy for the world and she'd tell you that herself if you ever bothered to ask. *(To MARIANNE)* Right. I'd better be off, then. We'll call back later. Just to check if there's anything you want. And remember what I said. If there's anything I can do...you've only to mention it. *(He gives her a knowing wink, then crosses to the arch and exits.)*

CARLA. *(after a moment)* So what were you *really* talking about when I came in?

MARIANNE. *(subsiding again, unhappily)* Oh, dear. I didn't want to say anything at the moment. It's too soon and it all seems…so *sordid.*

CARLA. *(caustically)* If it's anything to do with Frank Beverage, I'm not surprised. The word sordid was *invented* to describe men like him.

MARIANNE. *(uncomfortably)* Would you mind if we left it till later? It really isn't the time…

CARLA. *(tiredly)* It's as good as any. I won't be here much longer. As soon as the funeral's out of the way, I'm heading back to the States.

MARIANNE. *(frowning)* And what about Amy?

CARLA. We've not discussed it, yet. But once she's on her own, she'll not want to be saddled with a place like La Fenice. An apartment on Park Lane'll be more *her* style. *(Rises)* That's if she's inherited, of course. Knowing mother, she could have lost out to Save the Whales, or the National Trust. *(Moving upstage again)* I *did* love her, despite everything, but she was a law unto herself and used her money like a weapon. If you didn't do things her way, you were out of the will in a flash. But after I married Harvey, her threats just made me laugh. If she left me nothing, I could still have matched her, dollar for dollar. And that's why she hated me so much.

MARIANNE. *(shocked)* She didn't hate you, dear. She talked about you many a time.

CARLA. *(dryly)* I'll bet she did. *(Moves slowly left)*

MARIANNE. She told me how sad she was that things had turned out the way they did.

CARLA. *(flatly)* If she'd kept her hands to herself, they probably wouldn't have done.

MARIANNE. *(frowning)* I don't understand.

CARLA. *(wryly)* No. I don't suppose she told you everything. It wouldn't have helped her image if the truth had come out.

MARIANNE. *(blankly)* Truth?

CARLA. About him. The charming Mr Beverage. *(Stands behind the chair left)* We… used to be engaged.

MARIANNE. *(awkwardly)* Amy *did* mention it.

CARLA. And did she tell you why I ended it? *(Dismissively)* No. Of course not. She'd only know Mother's version, wouldn't she? *(Bitterly)* And his, of course. They could both be very convincing. *(Reflectively)* I was twenty-three when I met him backstage at Covent Garden, and it was lust at first sight. I couldn't wait to get him into bed, and that's where we were within an hour of leaving the theatre. *(A slight pause)* Does that shock you?

MARIANNE. *(shakes her head)* I'm too old to be shocked, dear.

CARLA. Mother was livid when I told her, but I couldn't have cared less. The more she raged, the more I dug my heels in, so when she realized I wasn't backing down like a dutiful daughter, she took it out on *him*. They'd had an arrangement of some kind. He went through her roles with her, and she paid for his singing lessons. Did you know that? *(Moves right slowly)*

MARIANNE. I had heard.

CARLA. Yes. Well that all stopped, and somehow or other, she managed to get him dropped from the chorus and out of Covent Garden, too. So a fortnight later I asked him to marry me. He hadn't a penny, of course…but I'd quite a bit of my own, thanks to Father's foresight, and gave him enough to buy a ring which I spent the next six months flashing under her nose at every opportunity. *(Matter-of-factly)* Then one afternoon… I had a dizzy spell out shopping, and came home earlier than expected. *(Smiles wryly)* They were in bed together…my *fiancé* and my *mother*. I couldn't believe it. She was twenty-five years older than him...and they'd been having an affair for over two years. God knows what I said...but the next thing I knew, I was on the floor at the bottom of the stairs with a broken nose and a split lip.

MARIANNE. *(shocked)* Oh my goodness.

CARLA. *(distantly)* The next few hours were all a bit hazy. I don't know where I went, or how I got out of the house, but I somehow ended up in a squat with a trio of drop-outs who'd found me in a side street, and carried me back. *(Moves down right)* It was the *girl* who fixed me up...re-set the nose and fed me painkillers... the men seemed to do nothing but keep a look-out, or scrounge for food or beer.

MARIANNE. *(concerned)* Didn't you see a doctor?

CARLA. *(shaking her head)* I crept out while they were all asleep and made my way to Dover. *(Reflectively)* I never even knew their names.

MARIANNE. *(curious)* Dover?

CARLA. *(tiredly)* For some reason I had my passport with me... and my cheque-book. I must have picked them up before I left the house, but I couldn't remember. All I knew was that I had to get as far away as possible. Somewhere he couldn't find me. And Italy seemed a good idea. *(Sits in the chair)*

MARIANNE. But... what about Tryphosa? Surely...

CARLA. She'd no idea. Or claimed she didn't. According to *her*, the last she saw of me, I was running out of the room screaming abuse and *he* was chasing after me stark naked. By the time she'd made herself decent, he was back again and apparently I'd gone.

MARIANNE. *(firmly)* You should have called the police.

CARLA. *(disdainfully)* To do what? I couldn't remember what had happened...not clearly, anyway. I could have tripped, for all I knew. But what I *did* know was I had to get away from him. From both of them. And that's why I ended up in Rome. With Guido Rinaldi.

MARIANNE. *(nodding)* And married him.

CARLA. *(amused)* Guido? No, no. There was never anything between us...except friendship. He was almost sixty, and the kindest man I even knew...apart from Harvey, of course. That's what made it so funny when Mother bought the villa to make us homeless. I'd have loved to have seen her face when she found out. *(Grimly)* But him. I couldn't believe it when I heard he was marrying Amy. I warned her, of course, but she wouldn't listen. She'd heard their story, and didn't believe a word of mine... Until the first time he hit her. After that... *(Gives a deep sigh)*

MARIANNE. *(baffled)* Why on earth didn't she *leave* him?

CARLA. *(scornfully)* Oh, at first it was all a mistake. A big misunderstanding. He only hit her because he loved her. *(Bitterly)* The only trouble was, he started to love her *more*. By the time she was thirty, she'd had more "accidents" than Charing Cross Hospital and I knew that one day, he was going to go too far, and kill her. So I made him an offer. Twenty-thousand pounds for every year he *didn't* lay a finger on her. Just one bruise and the deal was off. No hesitation and no second chances.

MARIANNE. *(shocked)* He didn't accept it?

CARLA. *(standing)* Why wouldn't he? Oh, he claimed he didn't know what I was talking about, but he took the money fast enough. *(Bitterly)* I paid him two hundred and sixty thousand pounds, over the next thirteen years.

MARIANNE. *(puzzled)* Then...?

CARLA. *(moves upstage)* The night after Mother had her so-called stroke and was rushed into hospital, Amy met me at the airport and I found out the truth. The beatings had never stopped, but she'd been too scared to tell me and became hysterical when I said I was calling the police. If I did, she said, she'd deny the whole thing. She could deal with it herself. *(Wanders* *slowly left)* I finally backed down, but cancelled the payments the minute I went home. He wasn't getting a cent from me in future. Then a few days later... Amy called. She'd been looking for headache tablets in the kitchen's medicine cabinet, and found something that worried her. A bottle of Haloperidol. *(Explaining)* It's a very strong tranquilizer. *(Stands behind the chair)*

MARIANNE. *(nodding)* I know what it is. We used it in the nursing home back in the eighties. It's highly dangerous and can cause confusion and seizures in someone who doesn't need it. And if it's suddenly stopped, it's also been known to kill. But what was Tryphosa doing with it? She wasn't psychotic.

CARLA. Exactly. And when Amy asked her about it, later, she said she'd never heard of it, let alone taken any. Yet the bottle was half empty. *(Sits in the chair)*

(**MARIANNE** *looks baffled.*)

So she looked it up on the internet. Amy, I mean. And found out exactly what you've just told me. That's why she called. If it wasn't Mother's, and Amy had never seen it before, there was only one conclusion. Frank Beverage had been trying to murder our mother... Whenever he fixed her nightly drink...and he did it *most* evenings, according to Amy...he must have been adding a spoonful or so to it...and eventually it had caused her so-called stroke.

MARIANNE. *(puzzled)* But why would he *do* that?

CARLA. For the money, of course. It's all he ever wanted. He didn't give a damn about any of us. He never had done. The only thing he cared about was getting his hands on Mother's fortune, and if he had to kill her to get it, then that's the way the cookie crumbled...

MARIANNE. *(stunned)* I can't believe this.

CARLA. Oh, he was clever, all right. But once Amy knew the truth, she realized what a fool she'd been, and how he'd manipulated her all those years. She couldn't prove anything, of course...he'd have denied it and probably given her a few more broken bones... but she asked for my advice and I was only too willing to give it. "Get rid of the bottle," I told her, "and if he asks about it, tell him you broke it by accident and leave the rest to me."

MARIANNE. *(intrigued)* What were you going to do?

CARLA. *(flatly)* Kill him, of course.

(MARIANNE *reacts.*)

I had a gun...Harvey insisted I kept one in my bag for protection and I'd put in quite a few hours at the range. I'd fly to London, shoot him, then take the next plane back with no one any the wiser. It was as simple as that.

MARIANNE. *(after a moment)* But obviously you didn't.

CARLA. *(smiling wanly)* It was just a pipe dream. I'd never have got the gun through airport security, and I certainly haven't the nerve to be a real killer. *(Rises again)* To tell you the truth, Mother solved the problem herself by making a new will when she came out of hospital. By leaving it everything but the house and a few bequests, she inadvertently stopped him making another attempt on her life. *(Moves upstage)*

MARIANNE. *(confused)* I'm sorry. I'm not following. Tryphosa left her money to the hospital?

CARLA. To build a new wing. Yes. *(Slowly crosses to right)*

MARIANNE. But Amy—

CARLA. Was still well provided for...though not well enough to warrant him making a second attack on mother. Which was why he got careless with his fists. *(Moves down right)* He blamed Amy, you see? And took it out on her. But Mother caught on, and no matter how much Amy denied it, just knew he was beating up on her. *(Pauses)* After he threw her down the stairs a fortnight ago, Amy spoke to me, and I decided there was only one thing to do. She had to divorce him before he killed her. That's the reason I came to Durning, as I told you. To make sure she saw a lawyer.

We couldn't prove he'd tried to kill Mother, but it would tear him apart if he were left penniless, and I'd definitely see to that.

(The door chimes sound and both react.)

MARIANNE. It must be Mr Perryman. He said he'd call. *(Begins to rise)*

(The chimes sound again.)

CARLA. I'll get it.

*(**MARIANNE** sits again as **CARLA** crosses to the arch and exits. A moment later she speaks again in surprise.)*

(Off) Amy? What is it?

AMY. *(off: distressed)* I heard it in town.

*(**AMY** enters the room in a dark mourning suit, followed by **CARLA**.)*

There was a fire. Last night. In Huxton Road. They've only just found his body.

CARLA. *(puzzled) Whose* body?

AMY. The man who lived there, they think. Mother's researcher. Mr Perryman.

*(**MARIANNE** reacts and begins to rise as the lights rapidly fade and the curtain closes to end the scene.)*

Scene Three

(A week later. Early afternoon)

*(The room has been tidied, and the flowers in the vase
have been replaced with others. The curtains are closed,
but outside, the sun is shining. A small stack of opened
letters and bills and a paper knife are on the coffee table.
After a moment, voices are heard off left)*

FRANK. *(angrily)* I told you it'd happen, didn't I? I *said* so.
Like a three-ringed bloody circus.

AMY. *(snapping back)* Well, what did you expect? She was
famous.

FRANK. They were standing on top of the *headstones*, for
God's sake. *(Disgustedly)* Bloody photographers.

(He appears in the arch followed by AMY, *who appears
to be in a state of tension. Both are in dark mourning
clothes.)*

Given half a chance, they'd have been in the casket
with her. *(Frowns)* And–

(AMY enters the room and crosses right.)

– who was the old bitch in the wheelchair with a nasty
smell under her nose? Who invited *her?*

AMY. *(icily)* If you'd taken any notice of mother's career,
you'd have recognized her. It was Mary Lassiter. Her
costume designer. *(Drops her handbag on the sofa)*

FRANK. *(incredulously)* You're joking. *(Enters the room but
remains left)* I thought she was long dead. *(Smirks
nastily)* Maybe she is. She certainly looked like she'd
been buried for the last ten years. And fancy Moretti
turning up. Haven't seen *him* since he conducted
Queen of Spades in ninety-eight *(Frowns)*...or was it
ninety-nine?

AMY. He flew from Berlin last night. With Zelda Bronski.
(Takes off her hat)

FRANK. *(surprised)* Hell's bells. Is *she* still croaking her lungs out? I thought she'd retired yonks ago. I didn't notice her there.

AMY. *(tossing her hat onto the easy chair)* That's because she wasn't there. *(Begins to unfasten her coat)* She's giving masterclasses at the Royal College. If she had turned up at the church, mother would have climbed out of the coffin and strangled her.

FRANK. *(sitting in the chair left)* Oh, yes. I'd forgotten. Not exactly bosom buddies.

AMY. *(sardonically)* Were any of them? Most had petrol cans in their handbags, in case the crematorium went on strike. *(Slips the coat off and drapes it on the easy chair)* Thank God it's all over.

FRANK. So what are we doing *here?*

AMY. *(moving to the window)* She wants a word with me before Carla goes back.

FRANK. *(puzzled)* What about?

AMY. *(tartly)* How should *I* know? She just gave me the keys and told me to make myself at home 'til she got back from the hospital. She was going there after the service ended. *(Opens the curtains in an irritated manner)* Why do they do this?

FRANK. What?

AMY. Close the curtains when someone dies. It's like a relic from the Dark Ages. *(Stands there looking out)*

FRANK. *(sarcastically)* It's called respect. Some of the old ones still have it. *(Musing)* Didn't look too good, did she? Hardly got the words out of her precious poem. And the look on her face when they played that recording of your mother's. I thought she was going to faint. Where the hell did *that* come from? I thought she'd never recorded anything.

AMY. It came with Moretti, according to Carla. Part of a rehearsal tape he made back in the sixties. Thought it might be a nice reminder of how good she really was.

FRANK. It certainly reminded the old girl. She looked like the Lady of Shallot when the mirror cracked. *(Concerned)* You don't think she's changed her mind, do you? About refusing the money.

AMY. *(turning to him)* Why should she?

FRANK. I could give you fifty million reasons. So how long will it take? Before we get probate?

AMY. *(after a moment)* Maybe months, according to Moretti. He went through it all with his daughter last Spring. It certainly won't be this year. There's too much involved.

FRANK. *(scowling)* And what do we do in the meantime? We can't live on my income. Not in a place that size. The bloody council tax'd take that, and still ask for more. Any chance of Carla opening her gold-plated chequebook?

AMY. I wouldn't ask.

FRANK. *(indignantly)* But *I* would. If we're sharing fifty mill with her, then the least she can do is cough up a few thousand to tide us over.

AMY. *(coldly)* Who says we're sharing anything? *(Harshly)* She's already got more than she knows what to do with. So why would she want my inheritance? Did *she* put up with Mother's tantrums for the last thirty years? Oh, no. She made damn sure she was well out of it. Well she can stay out of this, too. The money's mine, and I'm keeping every penny.

FRANK. *(frowning)* But Mrs G—

AMY. Has no say in the matter. Once she's refused what's been left to her, there'll be nothing she can do about it. And how will she *know*? She'll hardly come chasing after me to check.

FRANK. *(pointedly)* You *could* have a problem with *Carla*, though.

AMY. *(easily)* I don't see why. She knows she's been cut out of Mother's will, and isn't expecting anything from her estate. *(Smirks)* And besides…she's heading back to New York in the morning, and I've already told her that most of the money's been left to the hospital.

FRANK. And what if Mrs G *has* changed her mind?

AMY. I'll cross that bridge if I come to it.

FRANK. *(smirking)* Well…at least we don't have to worry about her turning anything over to Widow *Walker* and her brood, do we? Now Perryman's dead, there'll be no chance of that happening. According to the Chronicle, the place was a furnace. Whatever he'd found out must have gone up in flames. Hardly anything left but ashes. *(Reflectively)* Just shows, eh? Drinks and ciggies'll do it, every time.

AMY. *(moving left behind the sofa)* And by the way… *(Icily)* You don't have to worry about council tax. I'm putting La Fenice on the market and moving back to London.

FRANK. *(sitting up)* Hang on a minute. Hang on. Don't *I* get a say in this? I'm rather fond of the old place.

AMY. *(sweetly)* Then why don't you put in an offer? *(Pretending to remember)* Oh…of course. You won't have the money, will you? It'll all be in my name.

FRANK. *(taken aback)* But…we're *married.*

AMY. *(after a pause)* For the present. Yes. Though circumstances change. *(Brightly)* I could do with a cup of tea, couldn't you? How about putting the kettle on?

FRANK. *(rising with a scowl)* Never mind the kettle. What the hell's got into you?

AMY. *(suddenly seething)* I'll tell you what's got into me. You have.

(FRANK looks startled.)

(Accusingly) How long have you had heart problems?

FRANK. *(taken aback)* Heart problems? What are you talking about? There's nothing wrong with my heart.

AMY. Exactly. So why were there Digitoxin tablets in your drawer? And more to the point. In a bottle with Mrs Grayson's name on it.

(**FRANK** *stares at her, speechless. The doorchimes sound.*
For a moment, no one moves, then **AMY** *exits through*
the arch.)

CARLA. *(off, breathlessly)* Is she back yet? There's been a
change of plan. (*She enters the room, in mourning dress.*)
I have to leave in a few minutes.

AMY. *(following)* What is it? What's wrong?

(**FRANK** *sits again.*)

CARLA. *(turning to her)* Harvey wants me to join him in San
Antonio, so I'm flying home today. There's a meeting
with the architects on the new Opera House, and he
wants my input. I've just time to pack and get to the
airport before the plane leaves. Whatever it is, she has
to say, you can let me know later. I'll give you a call
the minute I arrive. *(Remembers)* Oh… *(Fishes in her
handbag)* And this is for her. *(Extracts a CD in a case)*
I had a copy made. It's Moretti's recording of Mum.
I think she'd like it. *(Pushes it at her)*

AMY. *(taking it)* And what about me? Don't *I* get one?

CARLA. *(frowning)* You can make another if you like, but
I never gave it a thought. It seemed a bit pointless if
you couldn't appreciate it. *(Glances at her watch)* I have
to go. But let me know if they find anything. It doesn't
make sense, does it?

FRANK. What doesn't?

CARLA. *(coldly)* Mr Perryman's murder.

AMY. *(surprised)* Murder? I thought it was an accident.

CARLA. That's not what they're thinking now. I read it in
the copyshop while I was waiting. According to his
assistant, he neither smoked nor drank…and the
pathologist found a few things that didn't add up. He
may well have been dead *before* the fire started.

AMY. *(frowning)* But who'd want to kill *him*? He couldn't
have had an enemy in the world.

CARLA. We *all* have enemies, Amy. *(Throws a dirty look at*
FRANK*)* The trick is to deal with them before they get

the chance to attack. Now remember what I told you. There's nothing to be scared of. Just don't even *think* of backing out. Alright?

(**AMY** *nods.*)

FRANK. *(scowling)* Backing out of what?

CARLA. *(ignoring him)* And don't be too long in visiting. You know you'll always be welcome. Thank Marianne for me. Tell her I'll be in touch. *(Hugs* **AMY** *and moves to the arch to exit)*

FRANK. *(sneering)* No farewell kiss for me, then?

CARLA. *(balefully)* I'd sooner kiss a rattlesnake. *(Exits)*

FRANK. *(amused)* Whatever happened to old-time charm? *(To* **AMY***)* I think you're right, darling. She don't deserve a penny. Swanning off back to the States and leaving us to deal with...

AMY. *(fiercely)* Shut up.

(**FRANK** *looks startled.* **AMY** *drops the CD case on the table behind the sofa and moves right)*

(Quietly) You were going to try and kill her, weren't you ?

FRANK. *(baffled)* Eh?

AMY. *(harshly)* You were going to kill my mother. With Mrs Grayson's pills.

FRANK. *(protesting)* Of course I wasn't going to kill her.

AMY. *(moving down right of the easy chair)* Then what were they doing in your drawer?

FRANK. *(giving in)* All right. I did take them. That first time we came here. I thought they might come in... handy.

AMY. *(raising an eyebrow)* Handy?

FRANK. If what the old girl suggested didn't work. Remember two years ago? When your mother was in hospital? If you hadn't been there for her, she'd have left almost everything to Covent Garden.

AMY. So? *(Moves round the easy chair and to its left)*

FRANK. So if she had another attack, it might have given her pause. A little Digitoxin mixed into her drink could have convinced her she'd had another stroke. Cut *you* out of her will, and she'd have no one to look after her. Unless she went the private nursing route, and we both know how long that'd have lasted. The nurse'd have killed her before the first week ended. *(Hastily)* I never *used* it, though. The mad man with the milk got in before me.

AMY. *(bitterly and almost to herself)* Another one in need of Haloperidol.

FRANK. *(baffled)* Halo – *what?*

AMY. *(after a slight hesitation)* Peridol. It's prescribed for psychotic behavior. *(Sneers)* My stepfather took it for months, but didn't know I knew about it. Stopped him doing too much damage to his stable boys when he was in a playful mood. *(Pointedly)* You might try asking for some. It's useful in the treatment of wife beaters.

FRANK. *(amused)* I might be many things, but I'm not a wife beater. Except where your mother was concerned.

AMY. *(Lightly)* And Carla, of course. Plus a few others. *(Moves up left, behind the sofa)*

FRANK. *(insisting)* I've never laid a finger on you. You know I haven't.

AMY. *(smiling nastily)* Of course I do. You bluster and bully and make demands. But no. You've never *hit* me. Though Carla wouldn't agree. Not with the evidence proving otherwise.

FRANK. *(blankly)* What evidence?

AMY. *(moving down to his right side)* The cheque stubs, of course. She brought them with her. To prove she's been paying you off.

FRANK. *(totally bemused)* For what?

AMY. To stop you from killing me. Twenty thousand a year, wasn't it?

FRANK. *(rising)* Have you gone mad, or is it me? I've never had a penny from Carla.

AMY. *(moving in front of the coffee table, pretending to think)* That's true, I suppose. You never even saw the cheques, did you? Whenever they arrived, I just popped down to the bank and paid them into our joint account.

FRANK. *What* joint account? We haven't had one for years. You said it was pointless. Your mother paid for everything, so there wasn't any need. You cancelled it yourself.

AMY. *(turning to him)* Nevertheless…there's almost three hundred thousand, in there. Pretty damning, don't you think?

FRANK. *(hotly)* Not if I don't have a clue what you're playing at. What's going on?

AMY. *(harshly)* I want a divorce, Frank.

(FRANK reacts.)

Your little game's over. I've learned a lot in this past two years. You've tried to kill mother twice, you *did* push Carla down the stairs in Hampstead, and I wouldn't be surprised if you set Mr Perryman's house on fire last week and killed him.

FRANK. *(astounded)* You're out of your mind. No one pushed Carla that afternoon. She tripped and fell. I tried to help her up but she was completely hysterical and almost scratched my eyes out. By the time I'd called an ambulance, she'd gone. And as for Perryman …why would I want to kill *him?*

AMY. You were hedging your bets. Making sure he never got the chance to trace Mrs Grayson's family in case she changed her mind about leaving her money to us. *(Bitterly)* You never loved me at all. The only thing you've ever been interested in is money.

FRANK. *(hotly)* That's rich. Coming from someone who's been conning it from her own sister for God knows how long with a string of bloody *lies.*

(AMY turns away from him.)

And don't turn your back when I'm talking. *(Grabs her arm and turns her back)*

AMY. *(attempting to free herself)* You're hurting me.

FRANK. *(furious)* No wonder she's given me the evil eye for the last thirty years. It's all *your* doing, you psychotic bitch.

AMY. *(fighting him)* Let *go* of me.

FRANK. *(harshly)* So you want a divorce, do you? Well you're out of bloody luck, and if you try filing for one, I'll sue for every penny you get.

*(**AMY** continues to struggle, then suddenly spotting the paper knife, reaches out, grabs it and stabs him.)*

(Surprised) Oh.

(He looks down at the wound in disbelief, releases her and puts his hands over it. She stares at him wide-eyed as he staggers back and moves unsteadily upstage left before turning to her with an effort)

Stupid bitch.

(He slumps and collapses behind the sofa)

AMY. *(after a moment)* Frank? *(Alarmed)* Frank. *(Hurries to the back of the sofa and bends over him)* Frank? *(Stands again and raises the hand clutching the paper knife dark red with blood)* Oh, my God. *(Drops the knife and backs away right, looking horrified)*

*(**MARIANNE** suddenly appears in the archway. She wears mourning clothes and looks very ill.)*

MARIANNE. *(entering the room)* Sorry I've been so long but— *(Takes in the scene and freezes)*

AMY. *(in a panic)* He attacked me. He was going to kill me.

MARIANNE. *(stunned)* Oh, my goodness. *(Stares at her, open-mouthed)*

AMY. *(gabbling)* I couldn't help it. *(Hurries to **MARIANNE** and clings to her, sobbing falsely)*

MARIANNE. *(faintly)* Have you called an ambulance?

AMY. It's only just happened. He was like a madman. *(Sobs loudly)*

MARIANNE. *(recovering herself)* There, there. *(Eases her away)* Let's have you sitting down. *(Leads her down to the easy chair left)*

AMY. *(sobbing)* It was the money. He wanted Mother's *money*. All of it.

(**MARIANNE** *helps her into the chair*)

MARIANNE. *(firmly)* Never mind that now. Just tell me what happened. *(She moves upstage and stoops to examine* **FRANK***'s body.)*

AMY. *(still sobbing)* It was after Carla went. She had to catch a plane. Something she *said*. About Mr Perryman. *(Fumbles for her handkerchief)*

MARIANNE. *(standing upright again)* Mr Perryman??

AMY. *(sniffling)* That he could have been dead before the fire started.

MARIANNE. *(frowning)* And...

AMY. And that's when I remembered. *(Mops at her eyes)* The night it happened. Frank had been out late...some kind of meeting, he said. But when he got home, he smelled of smoke. Not cigarette smoke. A sort of... wood-smoke. Like a garden fire, I suppose, and I asked him what they'd been doing. He just laughed and said it was a secret...then went upstairs to shower. *(Shakily)* Is he dead?

MARIANNE. *(looks down at him and sighs)* Oh, yes. He's dead all right.

AMY. *(sniffling)* So I asked him again a few minutes ago, and he started *threatening* me. Told me he'd kill me if I mentioned it to anyone. And that's when I realised it must have been him who'd killed Mr Perryman and burnt his house down. *(Shaking her head)* I should have kept my mouth closed, but I'd had enough beatings to last me a lifetime and I wasn't going to stand for any more. So I told him I knew he was guilty and was filing for divorce. He went berserk. *(Begins sobbing again)* Grabbed me by the throat and tried to strangle me. Admitted he *had* killed Mr Perryman, and not only that...he'd also poisoned you and Mother.

MARIANNE. *(puzzled)* But he *couldn't* have done. He wasn't even here that day.

AMY. *(mopping at her eyes)* He'd added it to the milk earlier. The day after he poisoned the supermarket bottles to throw suspicion elsewhere.

MARIANNE. *(stunned)* I can't believe it.

AMY. *(wailing)* How could I ever have trusted him? *(Sobs)*

MARIANNE. *(quietly)* I'd better call the police.

AMY. *(alarmed)* Do you have to?

MARIANNE. *(surprised)* Well, of course, my dear. The man's dead. There's nothing else I can do.

AMY. *(protesting)* I feel *sick.* I can't stop trembling.

MARIANNE. *(concerned)* That'll be the shock. A nice hot drink with plenty of sugar will do you the world of good. Just...stay where you are and I'll put the kettle on. I can make the call while I'm waiting for it to boil...

AMY. *(anxiously)* You'll tell them I didn't mean it? I was only defending myself.

MARIANNE. *(unhappily)* I'll...make you that drink. *(Glances at the body again, then exits unsteadily through the arch)*

(AMY sits in silence, head down. A few moments later, MARIANNE re-appears in the arch. She has removed her coat and hat.)

(Hesitantly) I know I'm being stupid, but you're quite *certain* he told you he'd killed Mr Perryman?

AMY. *(looking up)* Of course I am. Don't you believe me?

MARIANNE. *(helplessly)* It's just that— Well— Did he say *why?*

AMY. Because he didn't want him to find out where your brother's family lived. In case you gave Mother's money to them instead of us. *(Mops at her eyes again)*

MARIANNE. But I'd already *told* him—

AMY. *(Scornfully)* He wouldn't believe you. He didn't believe anyone. He told so many lies himself, he'd forgotten what truth was.

MARIANNE. *(distantly)* I see. *(Looks at the body again then pulls herself together and exits again.)*

(AMY sits there silently, working out her story. A few moments later, MARIANNE re-enters with a pair of china cups and saucers on a small tray.)

Here we are. *(Moves down right of the easy chair and proffers the tray to AMY)*

AMY. *(softly)* Thank you. *(Takes a cup and saucer and sips at the tea)*

MARIANNE. *(continuing down to the coffee table)* I don't suppose we should be in here. Not with— *(Her voice tails off.)*

(She puts the tray down, before taking her own cup and saucer and moving to the easy chair right, where she sits and closes her eyes wearily.)

Though it's too late to worry about it now.

AMY. *(hesitantly)* Did they say how long they'd be? The police?

MARIANNE. *(shaking her head slightly)* I didn't call. I thought you needed time to calm down. They couldn't question you now, the state you're in…

AMY. *(after a moment)* Will they send me to prison?

MARIANNE. *(opening her eyes)* Oh, no. No. You needn't worry on *that* score.

AMY. *(sniffling)* I mean…it *was* self defence. He did confess. And you and Carla can tell them about the beatings, can't you? *(Sips at her tea)*

MARIANNE. *(quietly)* Yes, I suppose we can.

AMY. *(sharply)* Suppose? *(Protesting)* But you saw my black eye. The first time I came here.

MARIANNE. *(nodding gently)* I did, didn't I? *(Sips at her tea)*

AMY. *(pained)* If *that* didn't look like a punch, I don't know what would. *(Sips at her tea)*

MARIANNE. It was most realistic dear. Almost a work of art.

(AMY looks at her in confusion.)

If it hadn't been for the greenfly on your cheek, I'd have been completely taken in.

AMY. *(staring at her)* What are you talking about?

MARIANNE. *(mildly)* You told me you'd worked for Max Factor before you returned to England. One of the world's greatest cosmetic suppliers. Yet you'd done such a poor job of disguising the bruise, it was almost as if you wanted it to be seen. Which *did* seem rather strange.

(AMY puts her cup down.)

Then when I brushed away the greenfly...I got make-up on my handkerchief. Not the normal kind, but theatrical make-up. It was none of my business, of course, so I kept my own council...but later on I began to wonder. If you'd fake a black eye...for whatever purpose...what *else* might you have faked?

AMY. *(panic setting in)* I—

MARIANNE. Then last week, Carla told me about the payments she'd been sending. To protect you from your husband's alleged assaults. And I suddenly remembered a very charming old lady in the nursing home I worked in before I married Gerald.

AMY. *(puzzled)* What?

MARIANNE. To everyone's surprise, she complained that someone had stolen money from her purse. It wasn't a great amount, only a few pounds, but she was in a terrible state as it was all she had. The police were at a loss, of course, so everyone in the home subscribed and replaced it for her. Two weeks later, it happened again. But *this* time she wasn't quite clever enough, and the missing money was found behind a picture in her room. Do you see where I'm heading?

AMY. *(glaring at her)* I haven't a clue. What's *that* to do with the way he treated me?

MARIANNE. *(sighing)* I questioned Carla again, later, and she told me she'd never actually *spoken* to your husband since the day she ran away. All the reports of what he'd done to you had come from you. And you were the one who told her he'd accepted her offer of twenty thousand a year to stop beating you. *(Sternly)* And that's when I knew what was going on. Frank Beverage had never laid a finger on you, and you'd been taking money from your own sister under false pretences. He'd probably no idea it was even happening.

AMY. *(scornfully)* You don't know what you're talking about. *(Rises)* And even if it *was* true, it wouldn't have mattered to her. They've got billions. A few thousand a year in my direction wouldn't even be noticed. So if you've any more ideas...

MARIANNE. Oh, I have, my dear. Quite a number of them. In fact, I spent most of last night running them through my mind. For instance—

AMY. *(tartly)* I've no wish to know. *(Moves up left)* You can think what you like. *(In mock hurt)* I've spent the past few weeks looking after *you,* a virtual stranger, while my own mother was dying in hospital, and this is what I get for it. Accusations and innuendo. *(Tearfully)* That man made my life hell and if I hadn't defended myself, it could have been me lying there on the floor. He was a vicious murderer.

MARIANNE. Really? And who did he kill?

AMY. I've already told you. Andrew Perryman.

MARIANNE. Oh, no, my dear. No, no, no. Frank Beverage didn't kill Mr Perryman. *(Pause) I* did.

(**AMY** *stares at her in shock.*)

It was your mother's fault, really. All that business about tracing her *real* parents. *(Quickly)* Oh, I'd no problem with *that.* That was her own concern. But when she asked him to trace *mine,* I'd no choice but to put a stop to it. The *last* thing I wanted was for anyone to stumble onto the truth.

AMY. *(staring at her)* I don't understand.

MARIANNE. Remember the cousin I told you about? Barbara Freeman. Well I wasn't entirely honest. She did go to Cornwall and vanish for thirty years, and she did make contact just before the fire. *(Sighs)* The thing that nobody knew was that it wasn't *her* who died that night. It was her cousin... Marianne Walker.

(AMY looks baffled.)

I wasn't expecting her, you see? She'd told me she'd think about seeing me again...but there she was, standing on my doorstep and looking like the wrath of God. I had to let her in, of course, but she wouldn't listen to anything I said. Just went on and on about how I'd let my parents go to their graves without ever finding out I was still alive, and how ashamed I should be. In the end, I just had to get away from her and rushed upstairs, but she followed me, still harping on about things I'd done or shouldn't have done. *(Matter-of-factly)* So I pushed her. The next minute she was lying at the foot of the stairs with a broken neck. I can't tell you what a state I was in. Tony had left me and the boys were abroad. To be charged with *manslaughter...* *(Shakes her head gently)*

AMY. *(realising)* So...you changed identities?

MARIANNE. Exactly. We weren't dissimilar in appearance, and she'd told me she lived alone. So I arranged it all to look like an accident and went to up to London, using her return ticket. A neighbouring farmer identified the body...or what was left of it...and the rest was easy. I put her house on the market, moved into a high rise apartment block, and found work in a local nursing home.

AMY. *(incredulously)* But surely *someone* must have suspected? Her bank, for instance.

MARIANNE. Why should they? I'm an excellent artist...
as you can see... *(Indicates the pictures)* so forging
a signature was a walkover. And I did take the
precaution of changing her account to another bank
when I moved home. Which is how I met Gerald, of
course. *(Smiles)* He was manager there and fell for me
hook, line and sinker. Once we were married, I felt
confident my secret was safe. And so it was... *(Bitterly)*
until *he* came along. Poking and prying into things
that should have been none of his concern. How
could I have known Marianne had an elder brother?
She'd never mentioned him. None of them had. And
suddenly they were there. A whole family I'd known
nothing about. A family who could have photographs,
letters, or anything to prove I wasn't the real Marianne
Walker. I almost died of shock.

AMY. *(protesting)* But you asked him to find them for you.
I heard you myself.

MARIANNE. *(dryly)* I could hardly tell him I didn't want to
meet them. But it was then I decided he had to be
stopped. When you left for the hospital, I dressed
again and went round to his house. He'd left his card
on the table, there, and Gerald's old car was still in the
garage, so transport wasn't a problem. I parked a few
streets away and walked the rest of the distance. He
was rather surprised to see me, but I gave him some
rigmarole about Marianne's German grandmother
and he offered me tea. It didn't take much effort to
doctor *his* with barbituate, and he fell asleep quite
quickly. After starting the fire, I slipped out again
without anyone seeing, and drove home. *(She smiles
contentedly)* He never stood a chance.

AMY. *(frowning)* Why are you telling me this?

MARIANNE. *(mildly)* I'd have thought it was obvious. You've
falsely accused your husband of assaulting you. Now
you accuse him of being the supermarket poisoner
and killing Mr Perryman. What more lies might you
dream up to justify his stabbing? The death of your

mother? *(Firmly)* Oh, no. Her death was entirely due to *you*, and I can never forgive you for that. The world has lost a superlative singer.

AMY. *(baffled)* What?

MARIANNE. *(accusingly)* You should never have told me I'd inherit everything if she ratified her new will. Over fifty million pounds. Money I never wanted or deserved. *(Rises)* Can you imagine my dismay? *(Moves up stage)* If I *did* inherit, the publicity would be enormous. My private life would be public property and who knows what the press would turn up in pursuit of a story? *(right of the sofa)* The only solution was to make sure she never got the chance to do it. The morning your sister took me shopping, I doctored the milk in the supermarket with Tylenol in a small syringe. Not enough to cause real harm, of course, but enough to promote concern in those who drank it. My biggest problem, however, was to make sure Tryphosa was thought of as simply another victim of the prank. And one who unfortunately died as a result. *(Smiles)* I fancy I managed that part rather well.

AMY. But you drank it too.

MARIANNE. Well, of course I did. *(Moves right behind the sofa)* But only after Carla rushed out of the room to get help.

(As she nears, AMY backs away from her down left)

Prior to that, I was only pretending. The moment she'd gone, I pinched your mother's nostrils until she stopped breathing, then sipped my own dose of the poison. By the time assistance arrived, I was just as ill as the rest of them. *(Right of easy chair)* You can imagine my fright when I heard they'd managed to start her breathing again, but fortunately she'd slipped into the coma that finally claimed her. *(Moving right in front of the sofa)* Poor Tryphosa. She deserved better than that. *Much* better. But what else could I do? I couldn't take the risk.

AMY. *(stunned)* You're quite mad, aren't you?

MARIANNE. *(turning to her with a frown)* I don't think so, dear. Perhaps a little more protective of my privacy than most people. But mad? No. I wouldn't agree with that. *(Sits again)*

AMY. *(wildly)* You're totally out of your *mind*. Sitting there like some benevolent Buddah when all the time you're nothing but a stark raving lunatic. *(Moves towards her with a screech)* You killed my mother.

MARIANNE. *(mildly)* And *you* killed your husband.

AMY. *(shakily)* Oh, no. *You* killed my husband. With your knife and in your house. *(Improvising a story)* I saw you do it with my own eyes...and that's what I'll tell the police when they arrive. We'd found out what you'd done, and you'd killed Frank to stop us telling. *(Triumphantly)* You'll be straight-jacketed before your feet touch the ground and you'll never see a *penny* of my mother's money.

MARIANNE. *(sighing)* I don't suppose I will, dear. Not that I ever wanted it. But I'm sure Carla will see it's put to good use.

AMY. Carla? What's *she* got to do with it?

MARIANNE. I got my hospital results just after the funeral. They've given me a month.

AMY. *(thrown)* What?

MARIANNE. Terminal cancer. *(Smiles wanly)* And I wasn't even aware I had it.

AMY. *(sneering)* It couldn't happen to a more deserving person.

MARIANNE. *(musing)* Four weeks. Hardly any time at all. Enough of course to make a will leaving everything to your sister. Including your mother's millions.

AMY. *(smugly)* Do what you like. I couldn't give a damn. I'll contest Mother's will or share it with Carla. It really doesn't matter. And once the police have heard *my* story, I know who they're going to believe. I'll give

them a call now, shall I? *(Turns towards the arch)* They
can be here in a few minutes. *(Sets off for the arch)*

MARIANNE. That's true. But *you*, of course, will be in no
position to talk to anyone.

(AMY pauses and turns.)

There was something more than sugar in the tea you
drank a minute ago. You should be feeling the effect
at any time now.

(AMY looks stunned.)

You had to be punished, you see? Not only for making
me kill your mother, but for all the *other* things you've
done. I couldn't bear to think of you escaping scot-free
though lack of proof.

*(AMY suddenly gasps and grabs at the chair left for
support.)*

AMY. *(weakly)* Ohhhhhh. *(Clutches at her stomach)* Ohhhhhh.
(Slowly slides onto the floor) Help me. *(Screams)* Help me.
(Slumps and lies still.)

*(MARIANNE rises from her chair and moves behind the
sofa to gaze down at her.)*

MARIANNE. *(slowly)* What a terrible tragedy. I arrive
home after the funeral to find you've murdered
your husband and committed suicide. I've no idea
why, of course. I'm simply an old friend of your late
mother, and was expecting you for tea. Perhaps you
could leave me a note? I'm sure I could manage that.
After all, it wouldn't be the first time I've forged a
document, would it? *(Nodding slowly)* Yes. A rather
good idea. *(Turns to move back right)* My best notepaper,
of course. *(Notices the CD and picks it up with a frown)*
Troppo signori. *(Realising)* Adriana. *(Turning to AMY in
excitement)* It's your mother's *Adriana*. *(Laughs in delight
then hurries to her player and takes out the CD)* Troppo
signori. Tryphosa Swan in rehearsal. *(Puts the CD in and
switches the player on)*

(As the aria begins to play, **MARIANNE** *sinks into the easy chair right, and sinks back to listen. For a few moments she sits there in absolute bliss, then the lights begin to fade as the final curtain falls.)*